This Book is Dedicated to

"The Teacher Of The Teachers," Eugene Fersen - SVETOZAR

By His Students

THE LIGHTBEARERS

INTRODUCTION

From the year 1904 until Eugene Fersen, also known as Svetozar, went into the Great Beyond on April 24, 1956, he lectured and taught the Science Of Being Teachings unceasingly throughout the United States, Canada and Hawaii. During his life, he personally taught more than 20,000 students, lectured before hundreds of thousands and reached many more who bought and studied the teaching he brought to the World. Some, after studying the lessons, went public with their own interpretations of these teachings by attempting to further advance these wisdoms. Still today, The Science Of Being Teachings are some of the most sought after books for those who are drawn to live the mastery of one's innate Divinity, as Eternal Living Beings.

This Book, "Advanced Teachings Science Of Being", contains unedited class lessons Eugene Fersen gave THE LIGHTBEARERS at the World Center from the 1940's until the Spring of 1956. Eugene's earlier lectures and teachings can be found in the already made public book "The Teacher," Vol I.

Advanced Teachings
in
Science Of Being

By Eugene Fersen, TL, Svetozar.

Originator, Author, Teacher of

"Science Of Being"

"The Star Exercise"

"The Mental Contact"

Founder of THE LIGHTBEARERS

and known to the World as

"The Teacher Of The Teachers".

Advanced Teachings

in

Science Of Being

Volume II

Published 2013 by

LIGHTBEARERS PUBLISHING, LLC

a division of

THE LIGHTBEARERS WORLD CENTER

www.ScienceOfBeing.com

ISBN-13: 978-0615919829
ISBN-10: 0615919820

Advanced Teachings Of Science Of Being, Vol. II

Contents

Baron Eugene Fersen

Baron Eugene Fersen was the eldest son of a Grand Duchess of Russia/Poland, known as Marie Olga Alexandrovna Medem of the Royal House of Medem and DeLacy—two of the oldest and most prominent of all bloodlines in the history of royalty—reaching back thousands of years. His mother knew before his birth that he was to be a guiding light for the people of this World; she called him *Svetozar*, meaning *The Lightbearer*, which he began penning publicly when he volunteered in the Russian Red Cross during the war. The Baron's mother saw to it that her son had the proper teachers and education that would assist and support the Absolute Eternal Aspects of his Soul so as to fulfill his divine destiny.

Baron Eugene was a direct descendent of Count Axel Fersen on his father's side and on his mother's, William The Conqueror. Eugene's uncle was Count Leo Tolstoy, the writer famously known for his renowned literary works *War and Peace* and *Anna Karenina*. Tolstoy was one of Gandhi's greatest influences and friend.

Baron Eugene came to the United States for his second lecture tour in 1904 to share his already popularized teachings and lessons known as *The Science Of Being*. From 1906 through 1921, Baron Eugene was investigated by the U.S. Government's Justice Department as a possible radical. He was teaching what the U.S. Government termed as 'radical religious thinking.' This investigation accelerated during World War I, 1914-1918. In late September of 1921, the United States Government closed their investigation. By early 1923, the U.S. Government allowed Baron Eugene to become an

American Citizen and granted him free reign to publish through the American Press, his already renowned teachings.

Before Baron Eugene was sworn in as an American, the presiding judge cautioned him, that once he took the oath to become an American Citizen, he would no longer be able to take the polish royal throne he was born to. Henceforth, Baron Eugene was known as Eugene Fersen to the American public, as Teacher and Author. Eugene knew his divine purpose and mission was not to reign over Humankind from a throne but to assume a modest seat of service for the spiritual progress of all Humanity.

Eugene Fersen was intimately associated with the world's most eminent teachers, scientists and philosophers. Some of his most profound personal teachers were from the lineage of the Great Magi. Eugene Fersen, 'The Teacher of The Teachers,' launched in his time the greatest 'Human Potential Movement' that would later become the inspiration for what he called, the 'New Age.' From the late 1800s, Eugene's teachings taught or influenced many of the great historical teachers: Charles Haanel (The Master Key System), Dr. Hotema, Elizabeth Towne (Publisher of Nautilus Magazine), Wallace D. Wattles (The Science Of Getting Rich and The Science Of Being Well), Edgar Cayce, Annie Besant (Translator of the Bhagavad Gita, Theosophist, and Leader of Woman's Rights), Huna Max Freedom Long (great teacher of the Huna ways and teacher to the founders of the Course In Miracles), Charles Fillmore (Founder of The Unity Church), Samuel Clemens (author of Mark Twain), William Walker Atkinson (one of the three Initiates of the Kybalion), Nikola Tesla, Manly P. Hall, Jon Peniel and the list goes on. Rudolph Steiner himself was touched by Eugene's teachings and had him as a guest speaker/teacher in the Steiner Schools whenever Eugene could be available. His exceptional and unsurpassed teachings continue to influence Humanity today.

Eugene Fersen taught anyone who had a genuine interest in the *Science Of Being*, the Truth, and the path to spiritual and human liberation.

At the time of his parting into the Great Beyond in 1956, he had personally instructed well over 20,000 students and at that time more than 100,000 people worldwide had read or been exposed to the teachings of the *Science Of Being*. These teachings today are regarded as some of the most inspiring literary works in the study and education of Quantum Science, Spiritual Science, Human Enlightenment and the study of the Soul.

Eugene came to share with us the Truth of these wisdoms with the hope that Humankind would free themselves from the myths that held them hostage and bound them to an un-liberated existence here on Earth. He shared that there are still vast amounts of profound wisdoms that remain veiled from Humankind because the un-liberated subconscious mind had become resistant to comprehending those truths. Eugene knew and had faith that as humans enlightened their bodies and minds and raised their Spiritual Vibrations as they lived in the physical world, more would be revealed to them.

Eugene Fersen, 'The Teacher of the Teachers' gave to the world with an open heart, mind and spirit these profound truths, his life's purpose, and his *Seat-of-Power and Privilege*. He believed deeply that all of Humankind regardless of race, class, creed, gender or difference should have access to these great wisdoms that were once only privy to the rich and powerful. He acquired, as he lived, the manna all alchemists are looking for, the peak of spiritual attainment. In that state is where one's body, mind and spirit reach Its highest vibrational aspect of spiritual evolution while living in physical form; where one's Spirit becomes One with Its pure Soul.

Eugene Fersen's life purpose was to bring to Humankind the lost principles of their first Primal Ancestors so as to assist Humanity to complete their task to awaken, to the All-knowing latent scintillating star that resides within each of their Absolute Eternal Souls.

The Lightbearers World Center © 2004

The Relative Heavenly Eternal Realm
Know Thyself And Thou Shalt Know All

When Eternal Soul, through Its use of Spiritual Energy benevolently chose Mind-fully to separate from the Graces of the Heavenly Eternal Realm and Its Superconscious oneness with the Great Principle – The Creator, a new "Bio-Neuro-Spiritual World," and a Solar System to support Its inhabitants, were artfully born in this Universe. These new systems were solely encrypted with all the wisdoms and Life Force Energy to support and nourish Soul's sophisticated yet subastral creation, as long as the skills to decipher and access the Nature of their algorithm designs was preserved within the lineage of Soul's Spirit as it lived in this new World.

Hence, the Souls that came forth from this phenomenon emerged in elemental form- crystallized vibrations as separate aspects of the One true Nature of their prior Divinity and began creating substance to support their mission; their purpose in a now material world. These now Earth bound Souls, backed with the help of "The Great Law;" and with the hope that Supreme Harmony would reign in their new world, believed they would achieve and prevail at their Earthly purpose and task to create a Heavenly Eternal physical world.

Souls that once inhabited the Eternal Realm aspired to experience the spiritual alchemy of a "Bio-Neuro-Spiritual World." There encoded and housed in these newly formed matter-bound Heavenly bodies, was their "Eternal Supreme DNA." These Souls outfitted with the profound aspects and abilities of their Supreme Eternal Nature encoded in their human DNA; backed with their divine intent, began to re-create collaboratively the nature of their divinity in this new world. Souls in the Eternal Heavenly Realm, the Realm of Harmony, never knew fear, aging, death, hunger, poverty, physical suffering, pride, hatred or lacked the power of Love - attraction.

In the Eternal Realm, the Universal Laws operate as one law and those laws are infinitely governed by three immutable forces called "The Great Law." But, here in the Relative Realm there would be altered aspects to the Universal Laws in relation to Soul made manifest in a physical world: First - that Soul, through the Eternal Force of Its Spiritual Energy would have access to and the use of Its Supreme Aspects of Creative Force so as to create what It desired at Mind's free will. Secondly - in the Earthly Realm, the Universal Laws that were once inseparable Eternal Forces became separate Eternal Aspects of their once united Heavenly Nature. And Thirdly – If Soul's Spiritual Vibrations are not in tune with the Supreme Nature of Eternal Harmony before reentering the Eternal Realm, then by way of the governing aspects of the Law of Attraction and the supporting virtues of the Law of Evolution, Soul would be drawn again to incarnate solely with the intent to liberate Its Spiritual Vibrations from the magnetic rhythms that bind Soul's Spirit to the material plane of existence.

As these Souls took root in the Relative Realm, they began to manifest and create life without a conscious understanding about there being a physical separation from their Divine Nature, the Universal Laws, their Creator or one from another. But this would change throughout their evolution. While these Souls forged and carved out their new world they simultaneously created energy-dynamic relationship with all that they had created through the Laws of Cause and Effect, the Law of Rhythm and the non-negotiable Immutable Laws of the Universe. They began to Love and worship the perishable instead of the Eternal and created Laws from untruths instead of embracing the Laws that once brought them salvation, preservation and Liberation.

Most Scintillating as a Brilliant Star was to be the prevailing aspect of the Eternal Mind made manifest. But, throughout time on the physical plane of existence, mind was deceived by Its own power and misplaced Its benevolent Truth, Divinity and Eternal plan. Spirit reuniting with Its Eternal Twin, Soul and awakening to Its Divinity, has become Humanity's age old quest for the unknown. To "Know Thy Self," as a living manifestation of the All Powerful living force of the Eternal and to make this Wisdom Law (Truth,) once again has now become Humankind's foremost aim and their mind's greatest challenge.

The choice to transcend the Physical Realm and return to the ways of the Eternal was a path never lost; there at the bridge to the Infinite is a gate that swings freely and at will between these Worlds. Still today it seems for Humankind, that there is yet a long road to travel before Liberation is realized and materialized on the Earth Plane; but with the help of The Great Law and the merciful aspects of the Law of Evolution and its loyal ally Hope, Humanity will prevail.

As more Light is shed on the Wisdom that is before me in the rare archival documents written and taught by The Teacher of The Teachers, Eugene Fersen, I have been shown that there has always been a proper scientific and spiritual term for our Earthly Realm. It seems over time, it has escaped Humanity's grasp to embrace and be-hold. Now that we have entered the "Sixth Race of Humanity," the race of the "New Age," where much Truth has been laid before the feet of Humankind, it is now suitable and a moral obligation to reveal what has been shown to me and from this day forward address this realm by its proper and All Powerful name, "The Relative Heavenly Eternal Realm."

I have come to fully understand, as I embrace my purpose, my Destiny as Acting Head Lightbearer for the Science of Being ~ Lightbearers World Center the "Why," I was chosen to hold the space of the Seat Of Inspiration for this generation – that I would in my time, carry out the most important virtue of its duty - to put forth the unpublished Wisdom left for me in print without reservation or withholding. I have intimately come to know the Baron Eugene Fersen by reading and being with his work since I was a child. I was taught by his words and by the actions of my Lightbearer Family, the deeper meaning of Truth and shown the depths and tenacity of Love. While Eugene lived, he eradicated the forces of the rhythms that bound the human Spirit to the polarities found in this World.

As I continue to unfold and put into print the rare archival information, I know without a shadow of a doubt that these teachings and other wisdoms still not yet revealed were never to be kept secret from Humanity. These unprincipled actions have created and supported a consumptive deterioration in the Evolution of Humankind. Eugene never referred to the Science Of Being Teachings as Esoteric or attributed their wisdoms to any one philosopher or teacher except for the Great Principle and for very good reason, as those statements worked against the Law – Truth. He taught The Science Of Being teachings freely, whenever one was ready to learn and wherever he was given the opportunity to speak about them; he did so with a devotional determination that was unwavering, until he went into the Great Beyond.

The Seat of Inspiration, the seat Eugene Fersen sat in, has been an immeasurable seat for me to behold; I do my best to honor my Destiny and purpose in a good way; with a great respect for All Life. For as many thumbprints that exist in human form and blueprints found in Nature, that's how many religions reside on our planet. The path that each Spirit must live to become One again with Its Eternal Soul and Its Creator is as unique as Its thumbprint. As I honor the incomparable you, I also honor your personal relationship with the Eternal and the path – the "Why," you must live so as to unearth your Divine Destiny and return to the gate that swings freely and at will between the worlds.

Written and Copyrighted by Laura Taylor-Jensen,
Acting Head Lightbearer,

The Lightbearers World Center © 2011

A Note For The Reader

"The Advanced Teaching in Science Of Being Vol. II," is comprised of unedited advanced teachings and class lectures given by the Baron Eugene Fersen in the early 1900's. Grammar, word usage, some scientific topics and the use of generalized gender pronouns found in these writings, are befitting and reflect the period before, during and post WWII academic style of that era.

The Lightbearers World Center's, Acting Head Lightbearers, would like to offer some insight to what Eugene meant when he used the following terms. We feel confident that these are accurate and proper interpretations. When Eugene Fersen used the term man or men in general it denotes Humanity or Humankind unless he was speaking about men as a gender type. The term problem connotes an opportunity or a task. When Eugene referred to the Father as the Great Architect or Great Principle in that statement, was included the sum of Its whole parts, meaning the Eternal Mother-Architect-Principle aspect was included and present. And Truth meant Law.

Lesson One

AGGRESSIVENESS

We need to be aggressive. Aggressiveness is found throughout the whole of life on this Planet, in plants and animals, as well as in humans.

There are two kinds of aggressiveness. When people are 51% right, their aggressiveness expresses itself in fighting for right. The more right the people are, the better their results. However, there is no human being who does not make mistakes.

Those who are 51% negative are aggressive, but because of their distorted minds, they express their aggressiveness in a destructive way. If their destructiveness can be changed to constructiveness, then their aggressiveness changes. Saul of Tarsus changed to Paul. When he reached the very limit of destructive aggressiveness, he suddenly changed.

A strong mind is always aggressive, either constructively or destructively. Nature does not tolerate weakness. It is the worst shortcoming in man or in Nature as a whole. Because of innate aggressiveness, all bodies in Nature have the power to counteract destructive vibrations. Those who adjust to an abnormal condition will later have much trouble adjusting back to a normal condition.

People who are inconsiderate, resent any consideration. If they remain long enough among considerate people, they will adjust themselves and become considerate.

Lesson Two

ANGELS

The mental realm includes all of the several planes in the so-called Beyond. Beings living on those planes, must incarnate at times into the physical plane. Those on the higher mental planes, incarnate only at very long intervals, perhaps a thousand years or longer.

The Spiritual Plane is the Realm of Harmony from which we fell. No incarnation from this plane into the physical is necessary, but Beings may incarnate at will, as in the case of certain Avatars. Such incarnating Beings must do so through physical mothers. This serves to lower their rate of vibration to the physical rate. They probably could not stand the materialization. They may project thought forms of themselves, which forms remain on the physical plane as long as the thought is held. These thought forms do certain work. This is the explanation of so-called Angels appearing.

Disincarnated humans, living in the mental realm, may materialize physical bodies at times, and do certain work on the physical plane.

The number of materializations and the number of angelic thought forms will probably increase as the veil between the physical and mental realms becomes thinner and thinner.

Lesson Three

BALANCE

Every question can be approached from many angles. In our present state of consciousness, there is no such thing as absolute right and absolute wrong. The middle path is one of balance. It helps us not to exaggerate. The middle path is not compromise, but a balanced position where we are not affected by either right or wrong. The Hindus, even in ancient times, said a balanced mind was one that was above the pairs of opposites. One who over emphasizes trying to do right, is unbalanced. Jesus said to be wise as serpents and loving as doves.

We should always balance love with wisdom. There should be no limit to love, but there should be a limit to manifesting it in a personal way. Otherwise we may unbalance ourselves in that direction. Love should be balanced by mind. There should not be a balance between good and evil that is 50% of each. We should only consider evil to the extent of not becoming subject to it, and not playing the game of evil. We should be very careful that the desire to do good should not make us do foolish things. Love unguided by wisdom can do horrible things.

We are today in the process of exposing everything. That which is supposed to be hidden is now being exposed. In the United States, these changes are much stronger than anywhere else. When the Country was first founded, the people were very balanced, but now we have become the most unbalanced country in the World. The people in the United States are very intelligent, but they do not use their intelligence, because they are mentally one dimensional. They are exaggerating everything to an unbelievable extent because of their insane desire for wealth and power.

There was never such a subtle manifestation as that which developed from the freedom of the press. This began to be used by unscrupulous people. Every line of advertisement is now a lie. Everything now is based on a lie. People do not think, but must have someone tell them about things through advertising. Advertising is now the foundation of everything, and advertising, as at present used, is a lie. A lie must be connected with a little truth. Truth is so universal, that there must be some truth in a lie. Truth is imprisoned. People, due to advertising, are so accustomed to exaggeration, that they do not know what Truth is. People have so much lost their sense of Truth or Balance that they are caught by lies. The bigger the people in business, usually the bigger the lies.

Exaggeration in the United States will be the downfall of this Country. To live on hot air works only for the time being. The leaders must be balanced. The masses from time immemorial have followed the leaders. We have lost our sense of balance and are just driftwood on the sea of life. The United States missed her Destiny, and once the Destiny is lost, it can never be regained, except after thousands of years when we again come to the same place in the Spiral of Life.

In the Fourth Dimension, we are so balanced that we are not distressed by anything wrong. It is a balanced condition which is above right and wrong. In a condition of balance everything is right. People with slimy minds always try to find a way to exaggerate. If we are determined to do something, nothing in the world can prevent it. That is the operation of the Law. If we cannot do it, then it is because it is not intended that we should do it.

Lesson Four

BODIES

We have within our physical body, a mental body and a Spiritual body. The physical body is not harmonious. It is a product of our subconsciousnss. It is subconsciousness in materialized form. The body must be first conceived mentally. It is in our subconsciousness, and our subconsciousness is very disharmonious. Therefore, the body is conceived disharmoniously. It does not come from our Higher Self. When born, it would be absolutely disharmonious if it were not for the Electrons which we use. Any harmony it has is due to our electronic structure.

Very primitive people have disharmonious bodies, because their electronic structure was controlled by subconsciousness. We have risen a little higher and have a better combination of Electrons.

Our Spiritual body is a manifestation of our Higher Self. It has a very definite form. It cannot in any way be affected by outside influences, because it is a Ray of the Eternal. That harmonious, Eternal body is the one which is liberated when we die physically. It is the Soul. The Soul is a very definite Spiritual manifestation. All Its activities, and they are FourSquare activities, are manifested in countless combinations.

When we are living human beings, our whole activities are based on the activities of the Soul. At conception the Soul is imprisoned in the very small body starting in the womb which later expands. If it were not for the Soul within us, there could be no life or activity. As soon as we are disconnected from it, we die. The Soul is the Unit to which we must look up. The higher our rate of vibration, the better the Soul can manifest through us. The rate of vibration depends entirely on Love.

Love is the Keynote to all vibrations. It is the Law and the fulfillment of the Law. It includes within it Law, Mind and Energy. This is why Jesus so emphasized Love. Love has not one of the undesirable traits of subconsciousness. It can never be irritated because it is unbelievably patient. Real Love spiritualizes everything it touches. It gilds and illumines everything it comes in contact with. It is never downhearted. It is always joyful.

True compassion is not a depressed condition. There is always a joyful element to it. It is so glad to have the privilege to help. There is a satisfaction that we can be of some use. If we are depressed, it shows we are lacking that Divine Flame. When we see something wrong, it should be only for an instant. Do not dwell on it. Say the good must win.

To be Spiritual one must find inner peace and harmony. If upset, always try to regain that harmony. Harmony always tries to get the upper hand of disharmony. The more we entertain or live up to the activities of our Higher Self, the more we give It the predominance over everything else, then the more harmony we have, and It gives an extraordinary Spiritual healing. The Soul bursts forth as a manifestation, and the person is healed.

In conjunction with the rebuilding of the physical body, we must try to rebuild the mental body, otherwise the healing is not permanent. Real healing is only when both the physical and mental bodies are rebuilt. To heal the mental is one of the most difficult problems, because we must deal with the silent enemy of subconsciousness. Subconsciousness must be impressed by the Higher Self, then it will work for us instead of against us. Subconsciousness does not want to be improved. The more unwilling we are to do anything, the more we are enslaved by our subconsciousness. Subconsciousness never admits that it is wrong. If it did, it would lose its power. Out Higher Self counterbalances and outbalances our subonsciousness.

Subconsciousness, having built our human body, would like to keep it undeveloped and sick. We must force it to submit to improvements. Subsconsciousness wants to be left alone because of its stubbornness.

There is no such thing as to be stupid. It means to have one's intelligence in a stupor. There is not one thing that comes to us that we cannot grasp, no matter how it comes to us, whether by reading or by lecture, or by any other method.

We cannot rebuild our Spiritual body. It is beyond that. It is a finished product. If the Soul could suffer or be lost, then, since It is a Ray of the Eternal, the Eternal could suffer or be lost.

If we want to bring about the best results in our conscious self, we should let the qualities of our Higher Self predominate as much as we are capable of for the time being. Demand for perfection comes from our Higher Self. A true perfectionist knows there are no complete ideals on Earth, but there are improvements.

In the human aura, the etheric double is the radiation of the Soul. It is about two inches wide and is invisible. Outside of this is the inner aura. It is the radiation of the subconsicosness and is also about two inches thick. The outer aura is the manifestation of the conscious self. It is from six inchers to several miles wide. The more the Higher Self manifests through the conscious self, the more the outer aura expands. The wider and more beautiful the outer aura is, the more that individual has conquered his subconsciousness.

The rebuilding of our physical and mental bodies is based on the foundation of our Higher Self. The Law of Harmony helps. It works through the Law of Evolution.

Lesson Five

THE BODY AS A FIELD

The Bhagavad Gita is known as the Lord's Song, and also as the Song of Harmony. It is the closest interpretation of life, as compared to Science of Being, with which I have come in contact. The following lesson is suggested by it.

The body is a field. It is for the time being, the field through which we have to function on this Planet. There is no other field through which any of us can function. This is why we should keep it harmonious. Some teachings try to ignore it, to despise it, to persecute it. This is a great mistake. No human can express the fullness of his knowledge through a sick body.

It has recently been discovered by medical men that the more educated people are, the more headaches they have. Our head is the channel through which our mind functions. What conclusions can we draw? If our knowledge were harmonious, the headache, if we had one, would be removed. The large amount of headache today indicates the large amount of disharmony. Leo Tolstoy (Eugene Fersen's uncle,) had plenty of headaches when he was young. When he grew older, and he lived to be 86 or 87, he had no headaches. He had great wisdom in his older age. He said that a person, who does not feel the depth of wisdom at the time of a contemplated suicide, has not lived a full life.

In Biblical narrative, Job reached the very depth of physical, mental and emotional distress. When he cursed the day he was born, which was committing mental suicide, when everything, even his friends turned against him, then regeneration started; first physical regeneration, then mental and then emotional regeneration. He cursed the day he was born, but he never cursed the Eternal.

Tolstoy at the very depth of his despair, when he contemplated suicide, started his upward movement. This is according to a physical law, which is that when we have reached the bottom, we can then start up. In diving, if we reach the bottom of the water and touch bottom, it is easier to start up than if we only dive part way to the bottom.

We should do the best we can to make our body a proper field through which to function. We are a triune being, body, mind and Soul. In a field we have the surface soil, the sub-soil and then below the sub-soil, the water. Any field that is properly cultivated must reach the moisture below. The top soil corresponds to our physical body, the sub-soil to our mental body, and the moisture below to our Spiritual aspect. The top soil has the least depth, so with our physical body. The sub-soil has greater depth, but is limited. So is our mind. The water beneath the sub-soil has hardly no limit. So is the Spiritual side of our nature. Without water, the sub-soil and the top soil would be useless. Without our Spiritual nature, our mind and physical body would be useless. The sub-soil has no effect on the water beneath, but it does determine the nature of the top soil. Our mind has no effect on our Spiritual aspect, but it does have a great influence on our physical body.

The Eternal, working through our Higher Self helps us to cultivate our field (our body). Our emotions are the water which make a barren field produce. Mind is a cold light. The emotion of Love makes the light warm.

Lesson Six

CAN FEAR HELP US TO ACHIEVE OUR AIMS? NO.

Fear paralyzes every power. If we are really afraid, we have no power to do anything. It paralyzes our ambitions. Dictators have a desire to dominate and to conquer. They do everything they can to counteract fear. If they were sure of their own power, they would be so harmonious that they would have no fear.

With poverty, there are two attitudes. Either we are afraid of poverty or we are disgusted with poverty. As long as we are afraid of poverty, it will attack us. If we are disgusted with it, we will have nothing to do with it, and will throw it off. People who are afraid of poverty, will have it all their lives. The thing that could prevent it cannot get through to help them.

In sickness, about half of the sick people are physically sick. The other half are mentally afraid of being sick, and so the sickness affects their body. People who are afraid of it, are the longest sick. Those who are disgusted with sickness, throw it off quickly. To be afraid of anything puts us into the power of the things we are afraid of. If we love or are enthusiastic about something we relax. We can only get rid of a thing if we are disgusted with it. Identification with fear is a natural thing for mortals. They have an unconscious fear before they are born, of what is going to happen next. That is why babies cling to their mothers.

Lesson Seven

CHARITY

Faith, Hope, Charity, and their Mother, Wisdom, the FourSquare. People do not understand Charity. It is not tipping. It means Love. If we speak with tongues of angels, and have no charity, it is useless. If we try to have wisdom, and have no charity, it is useless. John, the Divine, who died at a very old age, probably passed ninety, was often asked why he always said, "Little Ones, love one another. " He replied, "Because it is the greatest thing we can do." We have among civilized people, hardly any true charity on this planet. On the South Sea Islands, the foundation of their life was charity for thousands of years before the missionaries came and destroyed it. If we would have charity, we would not treat human beings as we do.

We have hospitals in various so-called charitable institutions, and calls for charity. Originally they may have been motivated by true charity. They soon became a formality, unless animated by sincerity. Very few doctors and nurses are motivated by charity. Most of them are in the work for other reasons. Cold mind directs science. There is no charity in it. People who contribute large sums of money may be sincere. Others, in large numbers, follow them for self interest.

Charity extends itself in every direction, because true charity understands. There can be no charity without understanding. One must be first wise.

Today we have, instead, sentimentality and a pollyanna complex. This is the reverse of true charity. Charity always follows the Golden Rule. It can be neither overdone or underdone. To develop charity within us is not easy. It must come from our Higher Self and not from our lower self. We find it among animals. They are very sensitive to their higher emotions. They are often very charitable to another animal or to their master.

Where are we to find true charity? In our own self. The more we are open to everything fine and beautiful, to the Gifts of Nature, the more the pearl within us of Love and Charity is shining. Charity must be exercised first on our self. Then later it multiplies and grows. It must be exercised on our own mind. Feed it with the proper knowledge and make it grow wiser. There should be charity to our own emotions. We should never use it in such a way that we would suffer by it. If we do, we would not be charitable to our self. We should never give to others more then we can afford to give our self. There is usually no wisdom shown in charity. Charity, when sincere, is very difficult to carry out properly. Andrew Carnegie would never give to any city library unless the city would give exactly as much towards the library as he gave. This is true charity.

One must be charitable within in order to manifest charity without. One of the fundamental principles of charity is co-operation. There can be no co-operation without charity. Labor strikes are not based on co-operation or charity. They are based on self interests. A firm and its employees should be like a big family and all treated in the proper way. Then there would be no strikes. If someone advocated them, it would fall on barren ground.

Charity should start in one's own self, extend to our families and spread until it covers the whole world. There will never be peace in the world until the true meaning of charity is understood. Confucius wrote, "Do not do unto others what you would not want them to do to you." Jesus improved the wording – "Do unto to others what you would want them to do to you." There is only one real sin and that is not to be charitable or Loving. There is only one Thing on Earth, which is really a sin, and that is not to be charitable or Loving.

Lesson Eight

CHRISTMAS, 1950

Christmas is a very memorable event in the life of Humanity. It commemorates the birth of a Being who was to carry the Message of Peace on Earth, Good will to Men. That was the Message, which He tried to live up to- to Love that which is good, thy Father, and to Love thy neighbor. There could be nothing more practical and idealistic. The Messenger tried to live up to it until His end.

The exact date of his birth is not known. Some say it was four years before the recorded date, some three years, and others have still different ideas. At any event, the birth of such a Being has not been correctly recorded. The dates of kings, of political events and wars, are correctly recorded, but that of the Great Being, is not. That is typical of Humanity. Thousands of churches have been built to worship that Being, yet His true birth is not recorded. Before the Eyes of the Eternal, it does not matter, but before human's who pay so much attention to the letter of the law, it is an unbelievable omission.

How can we commemorate a mistaken date? We commemorate a lie. When we start with a lie, we continue the lie. That little lie grew through the centuries. That is one reason why His Teachings have been so distorted and so misunderstood. Probably no other teachings in history have been so greatly distorted. The present Christians are so much less sincere than the first Christians, because that lie has permeated through those years.

We take great trouble to remember our own birthday and those of others. We are very particular not to miss the date. Why were we not particular to remember the date of Humanity's Greatest Friend? It is one of the greatest disgraces of the Christians. When scientist discovered that their calculation of the solar year was not correct, they adjusted the mistake. They could do it for a calendar regulating our material life, but not for a calendar to regulate our Spiritual Life, to commemorate the Messenger of Truth. You shall know the Truth and the Truth shall set you free. How can we know the Truth, when we did not try to learn the Truth of the birth of the Messenger? We cannot blame the masses. The whole blame is on the so-called spiritual leaders of Humanity.

With each commemoration of Christmas, the mistake has increased. In 1950 years it has reached a fantastic sum. This has no effect on the Spiritual Nature of us, or on the Great Messenger, but only on the consciousness of mankind.

The spiritual leaders who established the date of Christmas as the birth of the Messenger, made an unbelievable compromise with the Pagans on the date of the winter solstice. The Christian fathers adjusted as well as they could Christmas to a Pagan date. What a compromise! They wanted to have those pagans accept the new religion. It shows how people are willing to compromise even on Spiritual matters, if they find it advantageous to business life.

In the earlier years in the time of my boyhood, Christmas was entirely different from today. It was a family affair. There were gifts around the Christmas tree, which was a symbol of perennial life. The evergreen is a symbol of immortality. Christmas cards were written in their hearts. They knew that their friends would celebrate Christmas Eve as they were doing. It has now become the most outrageous business proposition in the World. All stores just wait for it, to make the most money they can. It is not Peace on Earth, Good Will to Men, but just greed. The sending of Christmas cards has become a nuisance. How can there be a feeling of Peace on Earth, Good Will to Men?

People have also put forth, instead of the Spirit of Jesus, the spirit of Santa Claus, and old fat man coming from higher regions. In days gone by, the messengers were parents. They brought gifts to their children on the sleds of their love. The children understood it. Now the parent's love is completely displaced by Santa Clause. The idea of parents' love was genuine. The idea of Santa Clause is a lie. In addition to the original lie of the wrong date, they had to impose on the little ones an additional lie. The children, when they find it out, never again trust their parents. The children and the parents were both more happy before the Santa Clause idea. The parents did not have to take the children before Santa Clause in a store window. There was true love.

We have now the worst Christmas spirit in a long, long time. We have more celebrations, pageants and dances, but the whole peace-loving race is agonized. Strange as it may seem, Christian Nations who think most of the hard time Humanity is going through, have transgressed the Principle in the most flagrant way. We will have more drunken people on Christmas Eve, more hypocrisy in the churches on Christmas Eve, more Judas kisses on Christmas Eve. That is the Christmas we have today. What can we expect from it? We will see what the people will get. We must blame the leaders in the material, mental and spiritual realms. President Truman, when he was asked to proclaim a day of prayer, said we already had Thanksgiving Day. His idea was that we can have too much communion with the Father, but never enough communion with the god of matter.

Should we discontinue pleasure? No, pleasure should continue, mixed with sorrow, as sunshine and rain. But there are times for everything, times for quiet and earnestness, times for joyfulness. Joy is that much greater when earnestness has been taken care of. Earnestness is that much more powerful when joyfulness is taken care of. We are now feasting and having good times in the country. We are sealing our own doom. An avalanche cannot be stopped. It will increase and increase until it reaches the bottom, then just destruction.

What shall we do? We are a small group of Lightbearers. We are a voice crying in the wilderness. We should commemorate the Advent on Earth of Humanity's Greatest friend, and the sacrifice He made. We should try to extend our love to those people who are just foolish and ignorant. Say, "Father forgive them, they do not know what they do." Let us not celebrate, but unite with our friends in the old way. Let us send all the love we can to a world that is fighting each other.

Lesson Nine

DAY DREAMING

The Teachings of Science of Being are not the teachings of the World. They are the Teachings of The Eternal. They are the Divine Road. We cannot switch back and forth between the two roads. With the welfare of THE LIGHTBEARERS is connected the welfare of the whole of Humanity. We will never understand this as long as we are humans. In The Beyond we will understand it. On Science of Being is resting now the future of Humanity.

There is only one right way, but millions of wrong ways. We are now engrossed in the physical plane. Unless mind is incorporated into Matter, we get no results. To make statements is one thing. To achieve is another thing. We must dare and do. We perceive many things which have not yet been manifested on the physical plane. No thing which is perceived intuitively can be prevented from materializing. The perception of it means that it already has been established on the mental plane.

Day Dreaming means building something for which there is no root in the mental plane. We must do something on the physical plane which will project itself onto the mental plane and become a new cause. There is a continual exchange between the two planes. A thing projected onto the mental plane grows there and increases in strength and power. On its return, it collects everything of the same rate of vibration. It is our own child which has gone to another world and returns a strong, healthy young man.

We cannot force the Eternal but we can be open to It. The best channel for the Eternal to flow through is our sincerity. In Science of Being everything is based on sincerity. When sincere, we cause high projections into the mental world, which is right around us, interwoven with the physical. Even the Eternal is pervading us through and through. An abscess is a wrong vibration implanted into the body, often accepted from another individual.

We are on Earth both to learn and enjoy. Most of us have to pay some debts of past incarnations. This is a prison. If we behave properly, we are paroled and have freedom to do more or less as we please. The Eternal never had plans for this. Our minds created it. Even reincarnation was created by us. The moment we establish the Law, we have to live up to it. We can get out of the situation. We will with the help of the Great Law, but we must do the right thing and stop day dreaming.

Lesson Ten

DECISIONS

Decision is one of the most important functions in our human life, both individually and collectively. Decision is one word, but there are many approaches to it.

1). Calmness. We need to be calm mentally and emotionally. Then not only can we reason correctly, but also our Higher Self has a chance to speak to us distinctly. Many decisions are a failure and a disaster. Failure means that we did not solve the problem, did not achieve our purpose, but it does not mean that we cannot stand up and start anew. Disaster means we have nothing left in us as a reserve.

So we must first find within us as much calmness and peace as possible, not swinging back and forth under the Law of Rhythm. We must not let doubt enter in. It is like a storm at sea, continually increasing and increasing. Another enemy is suspicion. It is a premature estimate of something we do not know. It is our own estimate, it may be very false. Another enemy is a quick temper. This is not easy to control, but it must be done sooner or later.

Many people think it takes a long time to become calm. Some people are by nature calm, but real calmness comes consciously. We should try to rise above the trouble. We can learn to remain calm in the greatest emergency and to be able to control panics. We can rise to the occasion in a fraction of a second. If we are calm, our Higher Self tells us instantaneously what to do. It works according to the Law of Demand and Supply.

2). Reason. After calmness, we must use our reason. This is true when decisions are not made in an emergency and by our Higher Self. Think over what precautions we have to take. Try to be as cautious as we can. Precautions should not be confused with fear. Fear nullifies our reasoning power. Caution due to fear is distorted. If we are full of fear we will never achieve anything.

3). Protection. Think as much as possible of protection. What protection do we have now and how far does it extend itself into the future, if we make a certain decision. Too much protection is just as bad as too little protection. Modern Humanity overloads itself with protection for little things, but entirely overlooks the big things. Do not lose ourselves in details.

4). Courage. To make a decision is to cast a die. When the decision is made, we cannot stop the result, due to the Law of Cause and Effect. We cannot make a decision without courage. The greatest mistake any human can make is to be afraid to make the mistake. We must have courage to carry out our decisions. Our motto should be "Dare and Do." Dare means to manifest courage. Do means to carry out the decision.

If we use the four approaches, we usually make the right decision. If not we learn to do better next time.

How do decisions affect human life? Take the present condition of the whole World.

First consider the peace conference at The Hague. It was a failure because people who were supposed to make certain decisions, did not do so. The League of Nations was a failure for the same reasons. The United Nations will probably be a colossal failure because of so much talk and so little decision. The United States is one of the greatest failures because of much talk and little decisions. The communist make well considered decisions. When once made, they have the courage to carry them out, and they do so in a twinkling of eye. The United States is full of indecisions. It is indolent, which means, I do not care. We became indolent because we did not train ourselves to be otherwise. We have a disaster in every direction.

Military we have been defeated in Korea by so-called barbarians whom educated people sneered at. In addition to the military loss, we have the loss of human life which we will have to pay for under the Law of Cause and Effect. Also we have lost the respect of other Nations, due to indecisions. Also we are bankrupt financially. This means, in the eyes of the modern world, bankrupt mentally. When we were pressed by the hand of fate, we, like any wild animal, fought blindly, and in so doing, every decision we made turned out to be the wrong decision. It will probably turn out to be one of the greatest catastrophes, and it will spread to other Nations.

What can we do? The die is cast. All we can do is not to become buried under the crumble of conditions. It affects our mind, our emotions, our health and the little happiness we are striving for on the Earth. This is a birdseye view of what indecision means on a large scale. In our own life we are versed enough in Science of Being, and intelligent enough to figure out our own decisions. Unfortunately we usually do this according to standards. This is due to our indolent character. It is easier to let someone else decide for us what to do. This is very evident in our clothing. We should not disregard fashion, but we should not be a slave to it. The best dressed women are the ones who make their own decisions about their clothes. They do not look like a wholesale dress shop.

People use slang because it is the fashion often not knowing what the word means. Very few people know the origin of the expression, "O.K." We always ask others what we should do. Then we do not follow their advice. We should consider what they say and incorporate their suggestions to improve our own decision. We should stand for our individuality and make our own decisions.

In view of present World conditions, we should come to one decision and that is to follow as much as possible what is given in this lesson.

Lesson Eleven

DESTINY, FATE, COINCIDENCE

Each one of us has our own Destiny, a blueprint and given to us, not only when we were born in this incarnation, but which is a part of our Eternal Self. When we were Spiritual Entities, each Being, whether human, animal, plant, mineral or anything which was a projection of the Eternal Itself, had given them a blueprint which they had to follow throughout Eternity. It was a perfect blueprint designed by the Eternal. Destiny is a Law of the Eternal. No one can avoid his Destiny. It can never be changed.

We may or may not live up to our Destiny, but sooner of later, we will have to follow it. The guidance of our Higher Self is the best way we can define our Destiny. Our Higher Self is the Guide which helps us to fulfill our Destiny.

Destiny is so important that the Ancient Greeks, who were some of the best balanced philosophers, placed Destiny above their gods. They realized that there was something above the gods which they made, and that something was Destiny. In the mythology of certain Northern Races, the gods were some day to pass away because that was their Destiny.

The Eternal Itself must abide by the Law of Destiny. Just as our Higher Self is subject to Its own Laws which it cannot violate, because such violation would mean Its destruction, so the Eternal cannot violate Its own Law which It created, because It would violate Its own Destiny, which is Eternal Life through Harmonious Activity. The Destiny of God is to be God. The Destiny of the Universe is to prove the Glory of God. The Destiny of all Beings, from the highest to the lowest, is to emphasize that Glory throughout all Eternity.

As we are living under that Law, we have the Law latent within us. Our Higher Self sees to it that we fulfill our Destiny. Each animal, plant, mineral, element has it Destiny which they must fulfill. When we as humans fulfill our Destiny on Earth the reward is peace and harmony, and in addition we have what humans call success. If we are a failure, it shows we are not fulfilling our Destiny. This does not mean success in the ordinary accepted terms. It means when we can say, "I did the best I can and am at peace with my conscience." Real success is that which gives us peace and harmony. It means completeness on the three planes. It must start on the Spiritual plane and go down through the mental to the physical plane. If started on the material plane, it usually dies on the material plane. We can judge whether we are fulfilling our Destiny by whether we find within ourselves the Kingdom of Heaven.

For one who loves plants, to take care of them is to fulfill his Destiny. One who wants to paint, and does it well, is fulfilling his Destiny.

Fate is something which originated when we became mortals. It has a beginning and an end. It is built by our own thoughts, feelings and actions. It is brought about by the Law of Cause and Effect. What we call the fatalistic attitude which some confuse with Destiny, is only the misconstrued interpretation of Destiny. Fate and Destiny have nothing in common. Fate can be changed. Destiny cannot be changed. No matter how bad fate is, since we made it, we can unmake it.

Some individuals are born seemingly under very favorable conditions. They seem to be "darlings of the gods." This is due to their past incarnations. The Ever-Present Now has the opportunity to make fate better or worse. We must learn to be faithful to our Destiny.

Coincidence is related to Fate. It is when two things meet, be they Beings, events or anything else, It is the result, through very complicated workings of the Law of Cause and Effect. Those who do not act according to the guidance of the Higher Self, have destructive coincidences. Meetings of people are often for mutual benefit. This is due to guidance of the Higher Selves. If we see that through the coincidence we get good results, it should give us great consolation that we are on the right path. We cannot blame some one else for a bad coincidence, because no one can change the operation of the Law of Cause and Effect.

We can become wiser by asking ourselves whether the latest turn of our lives, was filled with proper or wrong coincidences. We should be sure that we are fulfilling our Destiny. A person may have a change of heart. His Destiny overcomes his fate. The best known example is Saul of Tarsus, persecutor of Christians, who became St. Paul.

Destiny never acts destructively. It is the Will of the Eternal. Fate it does not violate this Law. It only interferes with men on Earth. No matter what wrong comes into our life, it is fate and not Destiny. We should fight it to the very end. Then we can say, "I have done all I can humanly do. It is now in the hands of the Great Law." Trust completely the Great Law and we will win.

Lesson Twelve

THE ETERNAL TWINS

Mind is the main subject, in a way, of Science of Being. It is both the creator and destroyer. In ancient India, it was Shiva, the Creator and Destroyer, the Positive and the Negative, the aggressive and the receptive, the blending of the two. Polarity reversed this, so that there is no receptiveness now. Instead there is a refusal to accept.

Constructive and destructive characteristics have been on this Planet since we came here eons ago. They are also present in animals, in plants and in the elements. Emotional and mental expressions blend into each other as the colors in the rainbow.

The training of our mind is the most important thing we can do. When we train our conscious self, we more and more train our subconsciousness. The true helper, the true guide is our Higher Self or superconsciousness. It is the core or center of the whole of our life. If it functions properly it affects our body. Accidents which injure our body, are caused by our mind. There is something in our mind that brings on the accident. The increasing accidents of today are because there is more and more disharmony in our minds. We come in touch with destructive vibrations. In the increasing World confusion, the increasing poison of our subconsciousness more and more troubles the waters of our conscious self. Look up to our Higher Self and It will more and more filter the waters and dominate of the situation. Start with little things and in time we can handle big things.

No matter how weak in character we are, we can always handled little things. As it is on the physical plane, so it is on the mental plane. As we grow physically stronger, we grow mentally stronger, and our character unfolds. There is a satisfaction and joy from doing little things. Each is a victory won. The more we perceive this joy, the more our sense of happiness increases until some day nothing but fine things come into our lives.

More and more people are now seeking improvement. Thousands of years ago there were only a few. It is not enough to seek improvement. We must stick to it. We must have loyalty to the thing we are seeking. It is not easy because subconsciousness wants to sleep and dream its own dream. Subconsciousness is not real, but only a shadow. The process is very difficult to start, but a blind wall has many doors. We can always find a way out. To find it, stimulates the mind. The emotional part of our nature is of great help.

This life is not an easy life. Each person has as much trouble as he can bear. We need sunshine. Even a little light helps us. Where can we find it? Usually we can find light in a very peculiar place, through our mind. Reason helps, but sometimes reason is not enough. We need love, that Love which does not know that anything is too great. Love coupled with Mind forms the Eternal Twins. When Humanity will have learned this lesson, it will have graduated out of the School of Life.

In everyday life, if we cannot lead others out of darkness, we can lead ourselves into higher ground. There is nothing more disheartening than to be disappointed in life. If we cannot have sunshine, then be satisfied with moonlight or starlight or manufacture our own light, a candle.

Lesson Thirteen

THIS EXISTENCE

We unconsciously think that things in the United States, and in the World, will by and by, adjust themselves. We are only now in the beginning of the trouble. Kids do evil things now just to get their names in the newspaper. If we do not steel ourselves against it, we will have that much more trouble when the big cataclysm comes. In days gone by the Light shone in the darkness but the darkness did not comprehend It, because the Light was gentle. This time it will be lightning, a mental atomic bomb. Now has come a time for evil ones to become more evil until they bring about their own destruction. We should fight evil on the physical plane by physical means, by mentally being more aggressive, and Spiritually with Universal Energy and The Sphere. I wish I could awaken within you, the fire of enthusiasm to fight evil. Betrayal is the most terrible thing under the Great Law.

Jesus taught Love, and utterly failed because Humanity was not ready for Love. Humanity is now ready for Truth and Law. I am Teaching this. Our worst enemy is a false sense of Love. The only a real manifestation of real Love on this Planet, is friendship. When the Corner of Truth is strengthened, there can be no up and down of rhythm.

We are living in a World which is a combination of physical and mental. Some diseases are physical and some mental. Those caused by physical germs are considered physical diseases. However, we would not take them if the original mental seed were not in us. Every germ has as its origin, a mental cause. Once the thought is incorporated into a physical germ, the germ has the power to reproduce on the physical plane without any mental cause.

Fundamentally we are Spiritual Beings. On this Planet we were originally mental Beings. Our original mental Being incorporated into the physical, and assumed all the characteristics of the physical, including self propagation. On the mental plane, our mental propagation does not consist of creating other minds. Instead we create thoughts. We're like a tree creating fruit. Our thoughts can multiply. On the Spiritual plane we create Spiritual characteristics which can increase, but we cannot produce another Spiritual Being.

The physical plane did not exist until subconsciousness was born. It has developed within itself, the power to multiply, and to multiply unreasonably. As an example, the offspring of a pair of certain insects, if not checked, would in time produce a bulk equal to the size of the Earth.

No animal mother will produce more young, at one time, than she has breasts to feed them. So when human mother should not produce at one time more than twins. There is often something in her subconsciousness which causes her to produce more, as triplets, quadruplets, etc. She does not have the breasts to feed them. She is devoid of reason. Reason is based on the sense of balance. Balance always goes with reason.

Mother Nature knows more than any of us, and more than subconsciousness knows. Nature never produces without providing for its subsistence. Subconsciousness goes against the Laws of Nature and produces monstrosities. In Ancient China, homes having more than twins, were cursed. In cells there is a natural multiplication, but there is always something which checks it when a certain point is reached. A cancer is fundamentally a mental and emotion cause which affects physical cells and causes them to multiply unreasonably.

Fear has power over an atom, but not over an Electron. The physical body can be cured if the mind is not poisoned by fear. In The Beyond, every mental and emotional feeling is intensified.

Subconsciousness is faithless. It denies Faith. In its essence it is disloyal to the Eternal. We are a breeding pool of disloyalty. When we are disloyal to others, we are disloyal to our own self. It starts with us, and then we are disloyal to others. Traitors fist betray their own Higher Self, and then their country. The atomic scientists are disloyal to science. Science is supposed to be for the good of Humanity, and not for destruction by atomic bombs. Inner beauty is based on loyalty to Truth, Wisdom, Love and others virtues.

Faith is the foundation of everything, the substance of things hoped for. With it, there would be no hope of the future. In present World conditions there is no faith in any direction. Blind faith is a misstatement. Faith being a Spiritual fact, cannot be blind. Love also cannot be blind. Infatuation is blind. Love has the clearest insight of anything. It is based on faith. The only One in whom we should have faith, is the Eternal. We then pay no attention to how humans treat us. We just ignore them.

Lips are so accustomed to uttering falsehoods that a smile does not mean much. Eyes never betray. No one can lie through their eyes. There is no poker-face in eyes.

We must be careful to choose that to which we should be loyal. To be loyal to the lower self, is the greatest damage to us. We must be pure in heart to see what is right. Only those really pure in heart will see the Father as He Really is, and contact and talk with Him.

Each of our incarnations consists of a greater adjustment to the Eternal. From time to time we are tested to fit into life. Then we discover to what extent we have improved. The main thing in life is not to adjust to one quality. That is not living the FourSquare. This unbalances us, putting one or more Corners out of balance. We are the key which must be fitted into the Keyhole of Life. When we are young, we cannot handle the key properly to fit into the Keyhole. We can each day be nearer the goal if we work hard in that direction. The Keyhole is Life itself. If we observe life, we find an easier way to adjust the key to fit into the Keyhole.

We cannot walk through the door of life by insincerity or pretense. We should try to do the right thing, but not to expect to succeed at first. No one is ever able in one incarnation to fashion their life and enter into the Realm of Harmony. We should never doubt that we will succeed by persevering.

Lesson Fourteen

THE FATHER

The word Father is so important because on that word is based the finest human conditions on Earth. If there were no prospective father, there would be no prospective children. If there were no children, the whole evolution would have been stopped.

The role of Mother is also essential. Mother is often likened to Earth and father to sky. Mother Nature and Father God are the same. From the sky comes rain which fertilizes the Earth, and the Earth produces everything. The "rain" of the seed of the human father, fertilizes the mother, and a child is born. This will be necessary for the continuation of the Race until a condition is reached where a new home, not the Earth, will be needed.

Since our beginning on Earth, the father has provided the food, and acted as a protecting genius to the children. Throughout history of Humanity, the father has played an important and sacred role. Through the worship of the human father, the people evolved and perceived that there is a Great Father, a Heavenly Father. All the greatest Helpers of Humanity, the Messengers from Higher Regions, spoke of their Eternal Father, who is Omnipresent, Omniscient, Omnipotent, Omniloving.

We are only asked to appreciate what the Father has given us in his Great Love. Only with the help of the Father, can we overcome, through our Higher Self, that lower self of ours. Think of the Father as air surrounding us. Without air we cannot live. Also without the Eternal Father, we cannot live. Breathe deeply of the air. If we take in the Eternal Father superficially, we get no results.

We are the living Temple built by the Father, in which His Power is residing Forever.

Lesson Fifteen
FRIENDLINESS AND CHUMMINESS

Friendliness and chumminess seem like twin words, but they are different as light and darkness, or good and evil. The word Friend should be very sacred to us in its meaning. When Jesus wanted to show the best relation to His Disciples, He called them friends. Up until now, the word friend has been placed on the highest pedestal. It was considered above a certain aspect of love. When the finest of any relationship is brought out, it is friend. We should be friendly to everyone but we should not throw pearls before swine.

Humanity realizes that a real friend is the most precious thing on this Planet. This has been true throughout the whole history of Humanity. The Pagans had friendship. Each human can have but one best friend. But if the power is great enough, it spreads and they have several close friends. There can be no jealousy because it is so beautiful. True friendship is sublime. It is always appreciated by those who receive it. This should not stop with only a few close friends. Those who are inspired by this feeling, have a more or less friendly feeling towards all. This is the pure gold that can be given and should be given to the whole World.

At the present time we have prostituted this. We have substituted the cheapest word, chummy. We pat anybody on the back to make them feel good, without meaning it. It is like a real piece of jewelry and a ten-cent store piece. Chumminess started in the United States and is spreading all over the World.

The right hand represents the power to do things. When we shake hands with a friend, it is like saying we cooperate with the friend in doing things. Now this meaning is lost. Chumminess seems to grow as long as things are favorable. When things go wrong, all the chumminess is forgotten.

The desire to be popular usually starts in school, and manifests more strongly in college. Those who succeed in business are usually those who are popular. Becoming popular is accomplished by advertising in one form or another. To be popular means to be chummy. What to do about it? We cannot change the World, but we should not let the World change us. THE LIGHTBEARERS are here to throw light on such things.

Chumminess is an imitation of real friendliness. People never accept imitations when they discover them. Some day people will not accept chumminess as real friendship. A Spiritual thing defies imitation. Real friendship is Spiritual.

Animals understand friendship. We all know of the friendship of animals to their masters. Often we find examples of true friendship between two animals, which are usually enemies, as between a dog and a cat or between as cat and a rat.

True friendship is above sex. Sex is the greatest urge on this Planet. The whole system of life in the United States is based on sex. I do not condemn sex, but teach that there is a greater difference between a material urge and Spiritual inspiration.

Krishna paid with his life for friendship to his people, but he had only one read friend, Arjuna. Buddha had but one. Jesus had John. These examples should make us understand the difference between friends and chums. Jesus had great dignity. He spoke as one who had authority. He was friendly, but never chummy.

None of us in this incarnation will see a real change in the World regarding chumminess and friendship, but it will come. Friendship is based on love, and Love is the Essence of the FourSquare.

Lesson Sixteen

THE FULL LIFE

We are in this life for a certain purpose. When we are born we do not know what the purpose is. Later we begin to see. Life is infinite. There are also no end of varieties. Though life is one, each must get out of it the most he can. That is the problem of each human, each animal, each plant.

What do we understand as a full life? First there is a physical manifestation. Then working through the body is an intelligence or mind. Then at the center and at the circumference, and all through it, is the spiritual aspect or the Soul. This makes the triune aspect, the body, mind and Soul. Unless the three are well balanced, we can never have a satisfactory life. A life that is not balanced is not a full life.

The fuller the life the more carefully it must be handled. It is like a full cup of coffee which must be carefully handled or it will be spilled. Everyone is intended to have a full cup of life, but each one has a different sized cup. It must be full to be fully enjoyed.

Why do people consider life such a hardship? It is not hard if we do the right thing. Materialistic people, if they put forth full effort, are materially successful. But they have filled only one-third of the cup of their lives. They often suddenly realize that there is something lacking in life. Such a life is one, which at the end of it leaves us disappointed. It is usually too late to take into consideration, the mental and spiritual side. Such people represent the majority of human beings. They are interested in what they eat and drink, how they dress and where they live. They think if they continually improve all this, everything else will be taken care of. They will be greatly disappointed. The size of the cup makes no difference, but it is very important how it is filled.

This is very difficult for most people to solve, because in the material world, the material life has to be taken care of. When we let the material or lower aspect take too much importance, we lost the proper perspective of life.

One of the greatest obstacles to our unfoldment is our innate jealousy. It manifests in countless aspects. In ever department of life, we find jealousy.

People try to camouflage it. It is not necessary to be jealous in order to unfold. Trees are not jealous, yet they unfold. Jealousy is so prevalent among humans that it contaminates animals and makes them jealous to a certain extent. The majority of people are very jealous. Because we are so materially minded, the things we are most jealous about are so unimportant, so transient, so little worthwhile. We are not happy, though we have material things we want.

The United States forgot the Principle of life. They attained riches and riches. They had no end of ambition. The atomic bomb was the last step in the wrong direction. It used the Power of the Universe. Man wanted to equal the Power of the Eternal. They said, "I am going to use You." This is where we are today. We all are to a certain extent participants. We have contributed to the downfall, consciously or unconsciously. Each over-reached in his own ambition. We have unbalanced our life. We have filled only one-third of our cup of life. What we prepared, we have to drink.

How can we make the best of it? Remember, we have not only a physical body, but also a mind and a Soul. If we are to live our life in full, it is never too late. We can work overtime. Our efforts will receive an overtime reward. If we balance our love and our mind we will be able to balance the physical side. We have not only the Principle of the FourSquare to balance, but also the three Planes, the physical, mental and Spiritual. When we make the right effort, we are not alone. All the Power of the Eternal is on our side to help us fight and conquer in our battle.

Lesson Seventeen

GOOD FRIDAY, 1954

Tonight the Christian World is commemorating a very important event, the Crucifixion of a Great Friend of man and a Great Lightbearer. It is very sad, and it is quite right that such a sad event should be remembered because that event commemorates not only that One who died on the material Cross, but also all great Friends of Humanity of the Past, who also were crucified, but perhaps not on a material cross. A mental or emotional cross is as great as a material cross. We must include all those who tried to bring Knowledge Aflame with Love, who tried to help Humanity live a better and a freer life. Many such are known, but the greatest number is still unknown. They should be remembered tonight because they died for attempting to bring Light to their fellow Beings. They were Lightbearers, too.

For thirty-three years, we have tried to bring to Humanity pure knowledge Aflame with Love, each one of us the best we know how. What is the result? The United States where Light was to be carried first, crucified us just as Jesus and his followers were crucified by the masses. Our tortures are mostly moral and mental, but they are hard to bear. In hanging on the Cross especially built for us by the people, because of their ignorance quite a number of us may cry out, "Father why hast Thou forsaken me?" In one voice all the Lightbearers may cry out the same. That is all we can say.

No matter whether we feel it or not, the Father can never forsake his children. So we must remember, no matter how hard it may be, we are only some of those who have been going through the same experiences for thousands of years. Yet not one of those tortures, past, present or those to come are in vain. Blood of the Martyrs of the Past water the ground on which blossoms of something finer could grow. So our physical, mental and emotional tortures are not lost. They have not been suffered in vain. Some day fine blossoms, the product of our work, will spring forth from that ground watered by our tears. We may say what is the use as long as we will not see them. Maybe from where we will be in that land of mystery, called The Beyond, we will see them. The harvest may be delayed, but remember when any harvest takes place, the one who sows the grain, partakes only of a small part of the harvest. The remainder is for others.

So if we present here will not partake of the harvest, because it will be a very great harvest, those coming after us, will partake of it and will bless those who contributed to make such a harvest possible. It is a test for us.

Those who do things, try with their mental eyes, to look into the future and see what good will come. The work is a slow one. The very minds of people refuse to accept a Message of Truth. It is a part of human nature, which was born in a lie and wants to remain in a lie. There are no end of alibis so as not to accept Truth. Yet in spite of this, Truth is bound to win some day. So remember what we Lightbearers went through in the Past, and are confronted with at present. It may seem like a dark hour. There is confusion even in our own ranks. Some others think of us as dreamy fools, as did the crowds 2000 years ago of Jesus and his followers. Still after a night, the day must come. We must cooperate like one big family, then can we stand all the negative, which like an epidemic spreads over the World.

We have chosen Friday as the day of our Assemblies. In normal times this should be a day of Joy when we can understand the messages of cheer. It now seems the darkest day. Yet we have chosen that day because of something deeper, than the sadness of crucifixion, the Joy of Living. Friday in ancient times was dedicated to Life, Joy. It was a day to the Good of life, the luminous God, who when everything else will collapse, when the older Gods will be no more, the God of Life will prevail. In anticipating a more glorious life, which will some day be in store for us because of our present experience, we chose Friday as our day for coming together.

The Christian World remembers Friday as a day of suffering. We Lightbearers try to remember something not sad, but something luminous, the Day of Light and Joy. This is very difficult in view of existing circumstances and World conditions. Still we must remember that Light, that Eternal Light, that Inner Light which nothing can extinguish, because it is a part of our Eternal Being and a part of the Eternal Itself. If extinguished, that much of the Eternal would be extinguished. That is impossible. Each of us has a spark of that Light burning within us, which can never be extinguished. We die, but the Spark never does. It comes with us when we are born again to become citizens of this World. It grows brighter to dispel the darkness of the World. It is known to us as Truth.

From time immemorial, it was considered a disgrace to tell a lie. Each time we tell the Truth we take a step forward to the Eternal Truth. The Light within us becomes brighter and brighter. If we let that Spark of Truth be covered by a lie, what value is life to us to walk in darkness? The result is self evident today. Ignorance believes it knows, because of its conceit.

In our Vibrations, we place in The Sphere of Love, all our enemies, conscious and unconscious because, in opposing us, they crucify us.

So let us remember that Friday before Resurrection, which is a symbol, and a great one, that when everything seems dead to us because of the coldness of people, someday Spring will come. Whenever sadness and trouble increase on this Planet, that which counterbalances all this negative, is also increased. We may not realize this, but it is a fact. There would be no darkness for us, if it were not for the human mind, which stands between us and Light. Our mind, opaque as it is, prevents Harmony from penetrating to us. If, we would turn our mind in the direction of Light, we would soon forget the shadow of darkness. Remember, in the process of climbing up the Mountain of Light, with each step we come nearer the Peak, with each step we are purified, and our characters improved.

Lesson Eighteen

GREED

One of the most primitive reactions, even in children, is greed. We see it in babies, we see it as they are growing up, and when they become mature adults, it is still developing. Humans usually have a very limited concept of its ramifications. Yet it is a big tree which started from a little agglomeration of branches. Under evil influences, even a branch of it can become a terrible weapon, a deadly weapon which can even kill love.

The usual aspects of greed are for money and power. Humans value power so much because of that unfortunate position in which we are today. When we were Spiritual Beings, the one who led those Beings to fall, was greedy for power. When those Sons of Light fell to Earth and became human beings, they wanted most of all power, but they had lost it. This was due to the Law of Retribution. Since those remote days the greed for power has become one of the most besetting sins of humans. This fight for power will probably continue as long as we live on Earth. This is the most important aspect of greed. Next to direct power, they want money to use to get power.

There are many other aspects of greed:

(A) At the present time security is very much in the foreground because we feel so insecure. Because of the way we feel we are greedy for security.

(B) We continually hear of breaking records. This is not the product of natural development but is greed. The people want more, more, more. They are not content with normal development, which would be pleasant and enjoyable.

(C) People are not satisfied to develop life on this Earth. They are greedy to go into regions far above this Earth with their missiles and their space ships.

(D) Fraternities and sororities are supposed to help students to bring out very desirable traits, but back of it is greed to make themselves better than the rest of the students.

(E) In military life, all the climbing up towards to the top, as officers, is greed.

(F) In social life, the social climbers show their greed.

(G) In family life there is greed, not for who is to be the leader, but for who is to be the boss of the family.

(H) A young man and woman before a marriage are greedy for the satisfaction they can get one from another. Honeymoons are a temporary triumph of greed. This means the death of love.

(I) A musician expects to be applauded. This is subtle greed for recognition. Applauding is supposed to give encouragement. Humans are supposed to have enough courage so as not to need encouragement.

(J) In the religious world there is a greedy climb from the humble ministers and priests up to the rulers in the religion, where there is more power to be exercised.

(K) Among holy men, some can honestly be called holy. The reputation is bestowed on them because they deserve it. But most so-called holy men are greedy for their immediate salvation. They are not human. There is no spark of love in them.

(L) Pictures in newspapers of brides and grooms are greed for publicity.

(M) Farmers try to get hens to lay more and more eggs, even though is means the early death of hens. They use chemical fertilizers to temporarily produce more and more crops even though it ruins the soil.

(N) Politicians would be willing to trample under foot their competitors because of greed.

(O) Outstanding persons of the world, the higher they rise and the more power they have, the more greedy they are for more.

(P) Badges and decorations for merit develop greed for more and more decorations.

(Q) People, who collect things of any kind, are greedy to have better collections than their rivals.

(R) Some families are satisfied with one child. Others want a dozen children. They are greedy so they can say, "What a big family I raised."

(S) Nations have most always been greedy to have a larger population than other nations.

(T) Jealousy is traced to greed. We are jealous because we are greedy for something, which someone else has.

(U) A person, who finally reaches opulence, usually forgets his friends. He still wants more and more. He will often give large sums to charity because he is greedy for the recognition it gives him.

(V) Alcoholics are such because of greed for alcohol. They cannot be satisfied with an occasional drink.

(W) Our over indulgence in food is greed.

(X) A person manifesting more and more greed in any form, becomes unhealthy because of the effect of mind over body.

We all have shortcomings, but we should not let them become masters of our lives. The whole of our life is an uphill movement back to the summit from which we fell. This climb should be harmonious, helping each other, but greed has obliterated every sense of decency, and we push and crowd each other. We are not patient with normal development. Greed is so subtle it sometimes hides under aspects where we cannot find it. It is one of the most difficult things to curb. There is nothing more deadly to Love than greed. Of course greed cannot kill that which is immortal, but it can imprison it very deeply.

Great people are by nature modest. They are interested in everything but are not greedy for them. The finest people are those least affected by greed.

Lesson Nineteen

THE GREAT BATTLE

Those people, who were unduly optimistic a short time ago, have now changed their views. There has never been in the whole history of the United States, and probably in the World, a more crucial moment than today. The United States is overly optimistic. Youth is always so. The United States does not have the experience and wisdom of older countries, some of them extending back for ten thousand years.

There was an Empire of Indians on this Continent. It was in a way a very advanced empire. We unfortunately did not credit them with an advanced form of government. Some Tribes, especially the Eastern ones, were very advanced.

History shows that our relation with the Indians was not a bloodless one, and was not a fair deal. We have been very unfair to the real Americans, the Indians. They were the defenders of their country and we were the aggressors. We did not even act as well as the ancient Romans, who were Pagans. They extended to conquered people a citizenship. We, a great Nation of Christian people, were deliberately unfair. Now we are in trouble under the Law of Cause and Effect. We must pay.

Another point. The Western part of the United Sates was a hot bed of outlaws, train robbers, murderers, etc. We must pay for this. The day of reckoning is now right here. Our present gangsters may be reincarnations of the older Western gangsters of the Jesse James type.

There is no question but that we have also done some right things. We have more churches than any country except Czarist Russia, but they give only lip service. We have more hospitals and doctors than any country, but we are the World's sickest people. We have more lawyers than any country, yet we have more crookedness. We have the best schools and universities, yet our education is the poorest in the World. We have plenty of theaters and amusements, but almost no good operas. We spend more money on our military forces than any country, but we have the poorest army in the World.

How can we win the big battle for remaining a great Nation? There are less than twenty-five chances out of a hundred of doing so. I warned of this years ago. Now the day has come. The people of the United States have some very fine qualities. They could have made, and perhaps will make, this a great Nation, but the people have not awakened. The people are immature, are children mentally. No Nation is more Pollyanna-minded than the United States.

Are we going to lose the fight? I am sorry to say that, as a Nation, we probably will. The pressure is increasing more and more. In addition we have the pressure of the whole World. The World must also pay its debts. The European countries may have partly paid already, but we have not yet begun to do so. When we entered the United Nations, we became a part of the mind of the United Nations. Before entering entangling relations, we made good progress, especially when we had good leaders.

Our own individual problems are now involved in the problems of the whole human race. When times are hard collectively, we must think of individual problems. What can we do? Others cannot do things for us. It is all so complicated, that in order to find a clear path out of it, we should rely more and more on the Principle of the FourSquare. Try to unfold It in our own life, and in our relations to other people, and to the World. Use fair judgment on World conditions and political conditions. We should not be connected with politics, but we should not be blind to what is going on.

The great fight is between two Principles. (1) Slavery brought on by the communistic or atheistic ideal. (2) The Principle of Fairness. In the United States we have made some feeble efforts along the line of fairness. The dark armies represent communism and the East, with a population of over a billion of people. This will probably be greatly increased in a few years, engulfing India, Africa, etc. They do not believe in a Supreme Intelligence, a Ruling Father of the Universe. It is to our credit that we feebly do believe in Him. So we are open to the Protection of the Great Eternal Father. He will help us to fight our battles if we will let Him. Therefore we have a tremendous help, but we must become conscious of It. We are on the right side. The communists are on the wrong side, and do not have the help of the Eternal. We should live up to the motto, "In God We Trust."

The battle is now between Humanity and the evil forces of the World, between Good and Evil. Evil is not all personal evil. There is also impersonal evil. There are those evil beings who passed away and did not regret their mistakes. They were born into the World of the Invisible, millions, and millions and millions of them. They are great units of power of evil. There are also invisible forces of good beings. They help us, in addition to the help of the Eternal.

There is not a greater power than All Power. Surrender to It and say, "In Thy Hands, I am placing myself. With Thy Help, Father, I can meet the situation."

Lesson Twenty

GRATITUDE

We pay the price for not being grateful for what we receive. There were twelve Disciples. One betrayed Jesus. He felt this so keenly that he committed suicide. The eleven remaining all carried the Message, but only John died a natural death. He had remained loyal to Jesus at all times, even to the end, and he lived a long life and reached an advanced development in every way. His last message was, "Little children, love one another." He died peacefully.

All the other ten died violent deaths. They tried to spread the gospel. Therefore, the work they did, which seemed to pay their debt of ingratitude, was not sufficient to pay it. For three years, Jesus had taught them, was their best friend, and gave them no end of acts of kindness. They deserted him at the end. Judas and Peter both betrayed him. Judas committed suicide. Peter thought he could get away with it, but he died a violent death. All ten went preaching and spreading the gospel all the years. This did not pay for their ingratitude and they got their punishment.

Ingratitude means betrayal. It is the worst mistake on Earth. Humans are now paying through millions and millions of years for one moment of ingratitude to the Father. Humanity is in a very bad fix now because they have forgotten the Eternal. Some do not believe that He exists.

Consider the current crisis between Truman and MacArthur. MacArthur is a representative of fine things and high qualities. We are going to pay a double price, first to the Eternal, and then to MacArthur. If we are not grateful to the Eternal, we cannot be grateful to our fellow beings.

MacArthur throughout all his life represented the finest that one could represent. Truman was an assistant of Prendergast, a gangster. Under the human law, assistants are guilty with the boss. Right and decency is represented by MacArthur. Evil in disguise is represented by Truman.

In the scale of justice, an individual is weighed as to how much right and how much wrong. People are a peculiar combination of good and evil. Most people are 51% good. The people who elected Truman are just as guilty as is Truman. People rely too much on other peoples' opinions.

This is the reason we now have the terrible rule of gangsters, which is a disgrace before the whole world. The method of handling the MacArthur affair shows Truman to be a gangster at heart. Truman will go down in history as the most despised man of this time. All who voted for him, will pay the price for this affair. As long as Humanity will follow the masses, they will pay the price.

We are already beginning to pay the price in Korea. There is an army of four million against our handful. The United States will not avoid paying its debt. MacArthur was the inspiration of his soldiers. The gangster took away the inspiration. The people will suffer.

People have a wrong concept of gentleness and weakness. Gentleness is not weakness. Weakness means weakness. Gentleness has in it all the ability to unfold. The Pollyanna attitude has done more than anything else to destroy the original fine qualities in the United States, because we wanted to be so kind and gentle. With Pollyanna attitude, no step can be done in the right direction.

In Evolution, there is a two-fold activity. If we act the right way, the Law of Evolution helps us in exact proportion. If we do the wrong thing, the Law still works, but it punishes us. The punishment is evolution, because when we are sufficiently punished, we stop doing the wrong thing, and this is advancement.

Why are we tired? Remember, we have our Higher Self which is never tired. Our lower self is always tired. When our Higher Self is overshadowing us, we never hesitate to do a thing, and we do it immediately. Today humans have turned their backs to their Higher Self. Therefore, the World is unbelievable tired. We are tired because the World is tired. The World is tired because it is tired of all the evil, for which we are responsible. This is a sign of Evolution, a sign of growth. It shows that we do not want to continue longer under this condition.

When people have achieved everything they want, they become tired of life on Earth. Some day we will achieve all that can be achieved here. Then we will no longer live here. This plane of existence will be no more.

Lesson Twenty-One

HALLOWEEN

Halloween started in the Seventh Century in Rome in celebration of the changing of the Parthenon into a Christian temple. Previously it had been dedicated to all the gods. The pagans in Rome and Greece were very tolerant to all religions. In one Grecian square there was an altar dedicated to the Unknown God.

Christians are supposed to be dedicated to the most tolerant worship of Love. This is not so. Halloween has become the very opposite of what it should be. It was originally dedicated to all saints, now to all witches. It is a day of ugliness, witches and pranks. Mind has deteriorated the day. A while back it was harmless pranks. It is not so now. Halloween was started in the wrong way. They substituted a fantastic religion for what the Parthenon was originally dedicated to. In thirteen centuries, it has degenerated into what it is now.

The Mardi Gras in New Orleans, in comparison, is usually good clean fun. The King and Queen are very beautiful. The grotesque masks of this carnival symbolize the ugliness of life. People laugh at the masks, and, in this way, try to laugh away the ugliness of life. Laughing destroys. I do not condemn laughing, but it should be used very carefully to destroy only certain things, which should be destroyed. Laughter is not smiling. We have never heard that Krishna, Buddha, or Jesus ever laughed, but they smiled. It was a smile of compassion and love.

Fun deteriorates the mind. Enjoyment uplifts the Soul. The United States must be a very miserable Nation today to be looking everywhere for fun. Halloween is a sample of our way of thinking. It could be wholesome fun without meanness in it. The present condition of the mind is one continuous Halloween.

The basis of the whole trouble is the ever increasing lack of love. Love cannot hate anything ugly, because there is no hatred in Love. All it can say is that they do not know better. Humans either hate or sympathize. Both are wrong. We love our own creation in Nature, but not Nature's Creation. There is nothing wrong with loving what we create, but we should not forget the higher aspects.

At the present time, pressure, such as World pressure, astral pressure, etc., is increasing more and more. This affects the nervous system, which in time breaks. Then it cannot control the subconsciousness. The subconsciousness then rules as supreme master. Insanity is when subconsciousness gets the upper hand.

Why is there such a diversity in the methods of suicide? Jumping out of a window means that the person wants to jump out of all the troubles and suffering of this life. They vision the window as an opening of escape. Shooting means that they are tired of their body or their mind and want to explode or tear apart the body or mind. Poison means they just want to go to sleep and never wake up again. All methods indicate a desire to escape this life, because it has become unbearable, due to lack of Love.

Only Love can heal a nervous breakdown. Love is the great harmonizer. It cannot be forced in us, but it can be developed. Start first with the little things. What people call Love is not Love. It lacks sincerity. We cannot express Love if fear is in our minds. Love has no opportunity to manifest if people are too intellectual. Professors today are not guided by Love, but by how much money there is in it. Love never sorrows about anything. It just Loves and manifests Love. It is not blind. It notices everything. It is the most penetrating, far-seeing and perceiving feeling that we have, because it is guided by Intuition.

Whatever we do, try to do it Lovingly. Then more and more of the good things of life will come to us. This is the Corner Stone of the Teachings of Science of Being. It is very difficult to be Loving in this loveless World. There is no other way but to conquer this condition.

It is not enough to contact Universal Energy as a Power. It must be blended with Love. When we contact It in Its aspect of Love, look up. Jesus always looked up when he "prayed," never to the ground. If we look forward, we face life as it is today, which is a very unsatisfactory life. If we look down, it is worse. The higher we look up with closed eyes, the nearer we approach the function of the pineal gland. We then feel very calm and peaceful.

Lesson Twenty-Two

HELP FROM THE ETERNAL

When one is conquering anything, that thing has already been overcome by the Eternal. When one finds opposition in conquering, he knows that he is right. We must do our part on the physical plane, after the Eternal has already conquered it on the Spiritual Plane. It is that much easier on the physical plane, because the Eternal says, "This is already accomplished, all you have to do, is to do your share."

We must stand up and fight, must be militant. We must bear the impact of trouble with fortitude, but we must fight it back. We should not put hatred into the fighting, but instead calmness, knowing that the Eternal fights for us. Fighting exhausts our human forces. We need to be inspired from above. We like to live a peaceful life, but we must till the soil in which we expect to build our future. The whole of life is a continual fight, but we are equipped to fight, and when we have done our part, the Eternal begins to fight for us.

The Everpresent Help of the Eternal is at our side. More than ever will we have to realize this. People forget that the Eternal is All there is. We can do anything within the Realm of Harmony, and with the help of the Eternal. When the presence of the Eternal is manifested, It outbalances destructive influences.

The Eternal says, "The Great Fight is My fight. Because I overcame it, so can you."

When we feel that we are at the end of our endurance, say, "It is already overcome, and with the Help of the Great Law, I can do it."

Lesson Twenty-Three

IGNORANCE

People change from one thing to another. To be constant is considered to be old fashioned. All Sages of the past asserted the very reverse. By many changes we can only scratched the surface. All great things are concentrated. The more superficial people are, the more diluted and deluded they are. Consistency means reliability. Constant people always live up to expectations, and can be trusted. The very reverse is true today.

Ignorance is when we do not see things as they are. It is not the lack of knowledge. It is either a conscious or unconscious refusal to know. Ignorance is a much deeper word then most people understand it to be. One can acquire knowledge, but ignorance is a deliberate step to see something and ignore it. No human can see and then say they did not see. Everything is instantaneously registered. There is no excuse for the mind to ignore what the body registers. We should be very alert in every direction, see, hear, smell, etc. The best way to begin is to pay attention. If a thing is good, we lose out by ignoring it.

Ignorance is not bliss. It is stupidity, the very limit of stupidity. No animal ever ignores things. It pays attention to everything. Ignorance is a curse, and a curse means limitations

Lesson Twenty-Four

INDEPENDENCE

On the biggest scale, true independence means living as much as possible the FourSquare Principle. This is balance. The more balanced we are, the more independent we are. Our greatest dependence is on the emotional plane, then on the mental plane, and least on the physical plane.

People are striving for independence on the physical plane. All Humanity throughout history has strived for physical independence, as for eating, shelter, etc. We start the struggle when we are born. We struggle because we want to live, and that means we want to be independent. In our quest for independence, we are forced to be dependent on some one else, or on something. A child has to learn to be dependent on its own legs. We will never have complete independence on this Earth plane. Even when we are completely liberated and have ideal independence, we will still be dependent on Universal Energy, Infinite Wisdom, Intelligence and Love. Before The Fall, we were as independent as we could be, but we were dependent on the Infinite.

Complete independence is only possible if based on something greater than our own independence. Everything depends on something. The ideal independence was dependent on Something Greater. Our quest for independence is an age-old question, which we have followed from Eternity. The thing that helps us to achieve independence is that which is greater than our independence, not lesser. A person trying to become wealthy is dependent on someone who is a channel for wealth.

Physical life must depend on a body, and a body on food, air, etc. No proper manifestation of mind or emotion is possible except through a satisfactory body. On the mental plane, the best way is to develop the FourSquare Principle. The United States is a living example of the struggle for mental independence, its escape from religious persecutions in England. We were an excellent example of mental independence growing from a few people into the richest Nation in the World. Independence must also realize responsibility, and we did not realize our responsibility. We are now more and more losing our independence. This is so, even of our own minds. We must have everything done for us. We have lost the urge for real independence. We are already enslaved. In other countries it is more or less the same, but they realize it and are protesting it.

Independence should not only be gained, but it should be maintained. If we do not persevere, we lose what we gained. Until we gain a condition of perfect balance, we will always lose, unless we persevere.

Independence or freedom is a great thing, but it must be properly understood. It can be based only on perfect Love. Then we will have the most ideal independence, and will recognize only our dependence on the Eternal.

When the FourSquare will be realized, we will become independent. No one can survive without the FourSquare Principle. It is the FourSquare Principle through which Universal Energy flows. The FourSquare Principle is the ideal independence. The more we live It, the more we become truly independent. The more we are balanced, the more we are truly independent. The FourSquare Principle balances.

Lesson Twenty-Five

INHERITANCE

There is a generally accepted belief that Matter, in the form of flesh, has hereditary traits. We must ask, which is more important, Substance or the Individual? The Individual must be more than the Substance into which he is incarnated. Scientists have found many traits, which at first they though were hereditary, and later found they were not. People cannot have a correct understanding of life and of heredity unless they accept the principle of reincarnation. Psychologists have not accepted it. They start at childbirth, or perhaps at conception, but never go farther back than that.

Individuals in The Beyond, are automatically attracted into the family into which they are to be incarnated. The family is the medium to the stratum, or class, or nationality, or race in which the individual is to function during that incarnation.

Each race has its own rate of vibration. The White Race has the more advanced race. Then follows in succession, the Yellow, Red, Brown and Black. Each of these races is unfolding, but they can also degenerate. The White Race is degenerating at the present time. This race has had many leaders in the Past, as Egypt, Greece, Rome, Germany, and England. Recently the United States has been the leader. Since the race is degenerating, and since the United States is the leader, this explains why the United States is degenerating faster than other countries. It is almost completely controlled by gangsters. There is something fundamentally wrong with it.

United States is now giving way to Russia as leader of the White Race. Leaders always draw to themselves those whom they are to lead. Russia has drawn to herself nearly half of the world population. The more advanced individuals in the future will undoubtedly be incarnated into Russia. The one, who was most responsible for the United States losing its leadership, was Franklin D. Roosevelt. He was the father and mother of the atomic bomb, the greatest destructive weapon of modern Humanity.

The Law of Vibration can never be changed. There is a seeming inheritance, but the Law fits the incarnating individual into the family, nation and race to which it belongs. The mother's thoughts and feelings during pregnancy do have a great influence on the prenatal development of the child. This, however, is not an inheritance so much as it is an influence. As a general rule there is no physical inheritance.

Lesson Twenty-Six

IS INSURANCE DESIRABLE?

If we would trust the Eternal to the extent of 51%, that 1% would be sufficient protection. But we do not. More and more I realize how little we trust the Eternal. The reason the negative has such a hold on us is because we are far, far below 50%. It is like the weather, which is sometimes stormy and sometimes bright. When we trust the least, it is like a stormy day. When we trust a little more, it is like a bright day. Insurance is only a human way to protect us, as long as we do not trust sufficiently in the Eternal. Jesus said, "Father, why hast thou forsaken me?" Even His Faith broke down. He who put all His trust in the Eternal, broke down. What can we expect from others, if such a beautiful example of unswerving Faith could not stand the pressure?

When I started Teaching, the Great Law offered me a very favorable insurance policy. If I had accepted, after 20 years of payments, I would now have a very large monthly income, and The Lightbearers would have inherited a large sum. I did not accept because I said to myself that the Great Law would protect me. It did to a large degree. I learned many lessons, but I do not think I would have lost much if I had accepted the insurance.

We live in this World partially spiritually, partially physically. It must be balanced, 50-50. If we balance it, we live a most satisfactory life. This is not so easy, but it can be done. Jesus solved the question very wisely when he said, "Give to Caesar what belongs to Caesar, and to God what belongs to God." We are not supposed to separate Spirit and Matter, because Sprit is involved in Matter. We should express in every act all of our Spiritual Qualities of Life, Mind, Truth, Love, or the FourSquare. To live a dual life, from the psychological point of view is very destructive. The end result is a complete breakdown. Churchgoers travel East, six days and West one day.

Life as it is lived by Humanity today, is a very unnatural life. In days gone by, long, long ago, when there was a seeming peace on Earth, people tried to live peacefully with each other. But the Box of Pandora opened. All the undesirable things in subconsciousness started to cause trouble. When all such traits are overcome, subconsciousness will no longer exist.

If we think of something right or wrong, we can materialize it. We can undo what was caused by wrong thinking by right thinking. Anything caused by some other cause, we cannot outthink it. To acknowledge wrong as something permanent is wrong. We should always realize that no matter how terrible the wrong is, we can counteract it by strong right thinking. But since we live on the material plane, we should also use material means. There must be a combination of Spirituality and materiality. Spirituality is not a way of thinking, but a way of doing. When we do a thing rightly, we do it Spiritually.

A thought that is not materialized, is not only undone, but we are punished for it. The Law demands the materialization, and if we do not materialize it, we are indebted to the Law. "The Road to Hell Is Paved with Good Intentions," is literally true. The more the intentions are not carried out, the more the punishment. People who spend much time studying occult matters and higher mathematics, are the ones who are usually least attuned with the Infinite.

Material life would be very, very easy if people would only love one another. There is a way to love people who are not loveable. Just leave them alone, and say, "I don't want to have anything to do with them, but I don't wish them any harm."

We should try to face the wrong the best we can by trying to think of the right thing. If we see someone unhappy, we should say that the unhappiness will some day pass away. People who know nothing of mental science usually do the best. Mental scientists are absolutely unbalanced. We are supposed to put as much Spirituality into our lives as we want to be Spiritual. If people would live what they are praying for, they would be much better off. On this Planet there is no way to avoid love. Everyone loves something. Some love whiskey.

To be FourSquare oneself is to be Spiritual. One who is a Spiritual success, can never be a material loser. If one can do the greater, one can do the lesser. On the material plane, there are two ways of gaining things, the right way and the wrong way. Therefore, to be successful on the material plane, does not always mean that he is Spiritual.

Life is a combination of Spirit and Matter. One who denies all material things is a loser, because he did not follow the spirit of cooperation. He gave away the material. The Spiritual does not demand giving up what is right. If we sacrifice something wrong, we are the winner.

We should never live in a dream. There is a great difference between living in ideals and in dreams. An Ideal is a problem to be solved, an Inspiration that shows the way, a thing that demands a realization. Love is the greatest reality in the Universe. It is not blind. It is the most deep seeing thing there is. That which is real, cannot be exaggerated. A dream is exaggerated. If we dream about beauty, when there is no beauty, we pervert beauty.

Enthusiasm, because it is such a tremendous power, should be used with the greatest care. Enthusiasm should continue to grow. Most people start with great enthusiasm, then it dies out. We should use judgment and see things as they are. The more we put truth into everything we see, the more Spiritual we are.

All life is a dream. In our individual lives we should not dream ourselves more into a dream. We should, instead, awaken from the dream.

The greatest handicap today is being in a hurry and thinking we do not have the time. If there is something we have to do there is always time to do it. Disregard the fear that we cannot do a thing properly. If it comes into our life, it means that the Great Law knows that we can do it, and that we have the time to do it. Jesus said when we are to appear before people, do not be afraid, the Holy Ghost will tell us what to say.

Lesson Twenty-Seven

JEALOUSY, HATRED, DOUBT

Real jealousy is one of the most disintegrating elements in the subconsciousness. It is very subtle, and an every-increasing poison in our mental system. It is based on fear. It can never be an incentive for anything positive.

If we are jealous of someone's possessions, we really hate that individual, and want to equal his possessions. There is nothing stronger on Earth than hatred. It is perverted love. Hatred lives in an individual until it consumes the individual. Reasonable competition is a very laudable form of expression. If it is based on a desire to outshine someone else, it is wrong. Athletes are usually very jealous of the achievements of their competitors. The fire of hatred is like an ordinary fire. If known in time, it can be extinguished. No emotion ever starts in full force. With human hatred, if we do not stop it, it makes us lose ourselves. It will never stop by itself. Greed is really the counterpart of the natural desire to grow.

Doubt is based on suspicion, lack of trust, lack of faith. Doubt paralyzes every constructive activity. Life is based on, "Dare and Do." We cannot dare if we doubt our own ability. "Who has ever seen the One who claims to be our Father and who is called God?" True it is that every morning a voice speaks within us, but there is none can tell whether it comes from our very selves (Science of Being, Page 311). This was the first doubt. The result was you and me, and the rest of Humanity. When doubt increases too far, one has to either kill the cause of the doubt or kill himself. We cannot find any other solution, except by rising above the doubt.

The contradictory power of doubt is Faith. Yet life is very strange. We cannot have faith in everything. Faith is one of the most precious gifts we have. If we would have faith, as children have, it would be so great that it would solve problems beyond unbelievable opposition. If we had enough faith, we could trust the most untrustworthy individual and he could do nothing against us. It is very difficult on account of our own shortcomings. Acts, not words, prove a thing.

Lesson Twenty-Eight

MENTAL DISEASES

Psychological trouble is of the human mind. We can only discover a comparatively few short comings of the mind. The moment a thing is exposed, it is conquered. To get results on the human mind is a very slow process. If we were to heal the mind, we would remove subonsciousness. This will be obtained only after many, many more incarnations, for some people probably thousands more. The majority of people have already come to this plane millions of times.

Most people are so completely under their own subconsciousness that they do not want to improve. Their Higher Self tells them to go forward and improve, to Dare and Do. Their subconsciousness is opposed. Since incarnations started we have had on this Planet a continual fight for millions and millions of years between good and evil, between the Higher Self and subconsciousness. What we know today of the body, mind and Spirit is already advanced enough to help us handle the fight. It is really a simple fight, but we make it complicated.

We should first make a simple denial and then try to feel loving. Self condemnation does not help. After realization of a mistake, bring out the opposite positive quality. All we have to do is to let the Law of Harmony work. We usually question, "Will it work?" A doubt on the mental plane causes it to fail. We have to be sincere and wholehearted. Whenever we hesitate, we lose out. We learn by mistakes. The greatest mistake is to fear to make a mistake.

Physical diseases caused by germs, viruses, etc., are comparatively easy to handle. They have no deep seated hold in subconscousness. Chronic trouble is due to some disharmonious cause, and is deep seated in the subconsciousness. If Universal Energy is really used, It works instantaneously, but we are too imbued with the concept of time and space. We find it difficult to free our minds of this concept. Therefore, it is best to use The Sphere and leave the whole problem to the Supreme Power.

Psychologists agree it takes a long time to get rid of one complex. If finally removed, other complexes may become prominent. This is too complicated to use in a satisfactory way. Universal Energy is able to arouse the Higher Self so that It sends all Its powers to get rid of shortcomings. This takes place on the physical, mental and emotional planes. The majority of people want to be healed physically, but do not want to be improved mentally and Spiritually. The reason most people deteriorate in health is because they are deteriorating in mind. We should keep the mind healthy.

In men, the mind is predominant and, since mind is very destructive, old men lose their beauty. With women, love is predominant, and old women retain their beauty better than do men. For the same reason, women live longer than men.

Lesson Twenty-Nine

THE NEGATIVE

The beginning of the great cataclysm is right here now at hand. Ordinary means of protecting ourselves are not sufficient. The enemy is the negative, coming from ourselves and supported by the negative in The Beyond. Astral influences can be described as the influence from Beyond. Those who lived a life 51% or more wrong on the Planet, when they die do not immediately change. The worse they are on Earth, the more hardboiled they are when dying, they are exactly the same in The Beyond. Those who do the best they can here, will continue the same in The Beyond.

The Christian religion, not understanding the Teachings of Jesus, has been more destructive than anything else. It has taught salvation by repentance. A mental or emotional repentance, not substantiated by acts, is worse than no repentance at all. The widespread belief that repentance just before death opens the Gates of Heaven is wrong.

Beyond death are two openings. According to our rate of vibrations, we are automatically attracted to one or the other. Those 51% right, are attracted to the right side. Those 51% wrong are attracted to the left side. Those on the side of right go into a condition of considerable improvement over their Earthly life. This improvement will go on until another incarnation. Those on the left side go into a condition where they will continually deteriorate.

Those who were 51% or more wrong on Earth and who thought they would be saved by repentance, will have the worst disappointment anyone could ever have. Their first reaction will be to curse the priest, or other person, who deceived them. Next they will curse the Eternal. The more they live there, the worse they will become until they reach a condition of such destructive vibrations that they will not be able to bear them.

There is no escape in The Beyond, so these negative beings revolt against such conditions, but not against themselves. They blame everyone and the Eternal for such a mental trouble. They cannot escape by suicide. They realize the terrible reality of no way out. We cannot realize what an unbelievable mental agony they go through. In their unbelievable distress they have to do something. They would like to attack those in The Beyond who are 51% right, but these have a protection and cannot be attacked. The more harmonious people are, the more they are protected. They also cannot attack each other because beings in The Beyond read each other's thoughts. They can only curse the Eternal, and then turn to the physical plane. They say they will destroy life on Earth, just as they tried to do when they lived on the physical plane. They start a deliberate war to the bitter end against life on Earth, not only against humans, but also against all life on Earth. Those on Earth, trying to do the best they can, are the greatest targets. This is the fight between good and evil. It has been going on for millions of years. No opportunity is ever lost to do as much damage as possible.

We should be cautions of a possible evil, but no afraid of it. Most of us are in a mental stupor. We have forgotten cautiousness which every animal on this Planet, and even plants, exercise. Cautiousness is a part of Nature, given to us to protect ourselves against a possible aggression. Since we are not cautious, it shows we are not intelligent. A suspicious person is afraid, but not cautions.

Try to be as calm as possible. This is different from serenity. Serenity is a wonderful quality, which very few people have been able to attain. It is a state of consciousness where the individual has risen above good and evil. They do good because they realize it is the only thing to do.

We must do our best and let our Higher Self penetrate into our consciousness more than our subconsciousness penetrates into our conscious self. Before going to bed each night, and after getting into bed and just before going to sleep, I use the closing vibrations given at our Assemblies. I feel this is the only thing that will protect us in the great cataclysm, which is starting now.

Lesson Thirty

PASSING OF THE LIGHT

In the most remote period of Light Itself, the Eternal Itself was and is The Light. Our Father is the Eternal Light. The Eternal Light bore Its own Eternal Light to the Universe. It said to the Light, Let There Be Light, and There Was Light. This is a human interpretation of a fact that never started, and will never come to an end. The Light is our most glorious Gift from The Father. It is Love.

Before our tragic Fall, we were full of that Light. Each time we did something or felt or said something to another Being, we were Lightbearers. We passed the Light to them. When we turned from The Light, still there was Light within us, waiting for the time when we would analyze our inner self, and would discover that there is an inner Light which we had not been aware of.

From time to time when darkness seemed to prevail on Earth, then for the destruction of evil, for the protection of good, a Messenger of Love would come carrying The Light with him. Because the human mind, since its Fall, was opposed to Light, it fought the Messenger of Love. The fight still goes on and will grow.

Science of Being, because of Its printed form, will probably remain on this Earth, as long as Humanity is here. It is a Message of Light, Aflame with Love. The Spirit of Truth is here NOW in a visible form as a book. The Eternal says to the Book, "Go into the World, live among the children of the World and bear to them the Message of Truth and Love, the True Message Aflame with Love."

Who are the Lightbearers of the World? Everything that has eyes. In the eyes is seen the expression of the Soul. Animals, especially friendly ones, express love to us. Even plants have embodied in them, the power of perception. The Passing of Light or Love will go on throughout Eternity. When a fellow being looks at us in a friendly way, he is passing the Light to us, which we, like a mirror, reflect back. When we look at an animal, remember they also have an Inner Light, and that the Eternal made them Lightbearers to the World. It is the same with plants, especially in the Spring, at the time they burst forth, they are sending us a Message of Love.

They are Lightbearers to us. When we look at a stone, we can always find some beauty in it. It becomes a Lightbearer to us, carrying the Message to us. Water, beautiful springs, river, waterfalls, lakes, the ocean itself, bears to us a Message of Love.

It is a Lightbearer to us. Everybody and everything is a Lightbearer. We like to have animals and plants around us because we want little Lightbearers around us. There is nothing greater than to be Lightbearers.

Our Centers are called Towers, to show that they are above others. Anything that towers above others is that much nearer to the Eternal. In this present Age, the Passing of The Light is a most important thing because The Light within us is damned up by our lack of Love. The Passing of The Light in our Centers, together with our lessons, is to keep The Light Burning.

At The Passing of The Light, there is a Spiritual Event taking place, if we do it with the proper Spirit. When we pass it, we also pass it to the whole World. As many as will receive It, that many will take a great step towards the day when they will realize Eternal Light within and without.

Lesson Thirty-One

PATIENCE

In the present condition of the World, people more and more realize that something constructive has to be done. They don't know what. They are waiting, both collectively and individually for something constructive to happen. Each of us has two problems, ourselves and the World at large. If we can handle the problems for ourselves, we can perhaps by thought, handle our surroundings. What are the main traits of our character which we have to put into operation? Energy, wisdom, sincerity and harmony. These are the FourSquare Principle, the foundation on which we embroider the pattern of our life.

In embroidery there is only one way to make a right stitch, but countless ways to make wrong stitches. In life we know what is the right stitch, and we should follow it. There is no better way than the right stitch. In embroidery we cannot make new stitches over a wrong stitch. In life, if we make a mistake, we cannot cover it over with the right thing. We are never the final victims of a mistake. We can always undo the mistake. Mistakes must be dematerialized. They cannot be patched up. They must be undone, and then replaced with the right thing.

People say they cannot do a thing because they are not qualified. There is not one person who is not given at birth given at birth all the necessary qualities to embroider the pattern of his own individual life. They are either too lazy or they do not understand. They throw the blame on others, or even on the Eternal, instead of on themselves. It is harder for those more richly endowed to learn this lesson than for those less richly endowed. The richer endowed we are, the more particular we must be. The more valuable things are in life, the more patient we should be trying to work them out.

The aim of Humanity nowadays is to save effort, time, and money. In every direction there are ways to do things with great speed. There is no quality today. Everything is scientifically "doctored up," even foods. Science wants to impose its own mental gymnastics on the Laws of Nature in every direction. Even chemical fertilization of soil is not satisfactory. Humans are so impatient. The laws of nature are very patient. We should understand this. We cannot have everything in life in a jiffy. Science of

Being cannot be learned overnight. It has to be assimilated. The so-called instantaneous healings are not instantaneous. There was preparation for the healing, deep within the person for a long time. The method, which brought about the healing, came at just the right time, when the person was ready for it.

Objects of art, which have lasted through the centuries, were worked out with great patience. People do not want to be patient. Without patience, they will never succeed. We are accustomed to live in an excessive tempo of life. As a result, we die prematurely, without enjoying life. We rush to do things, rush to die. Modern life has given a perspective of quicker death. People say we are prolonging life. What a joke!

It is difficult to be patient on things that are wrong. Patience feeds itself on things that are right, and destroys itself on things that are wrong. In the present World condition, Humanity was patient at the wrong time. We should have been impatient to protect ourselves when there was time enough to do it. It is now almost too late so we are in a dilemma. As it is in a general way, so it is in our individual way. We should ponder each day what is to be done, and how to do it. We should ponder whether it is worthwhile daring. If there is no chance, the effort will be just wasted.

We should not try to reform an individual. Let each one work it out for himself. If he asks for help, never refuse, but never impose it on others.

What can we do now? We used patience in the wrong way. We must now use it in the right way. As we have been patient in foolishness, so must we now be in our wisdom. This will improve our character. Say that we brought on the trouble and we must be patient to work it out. Always look forward to constructive results. We can do plenty for our selves, if not for Humanity.

Lesson Thirty-Two

PEACE AND WAR

This subject is very timely today, but the roots are in the far, far past. Wars started when Humanity came into being on this Planet. According to the Law of Rhythm, peace had to follow war. It is the pendulum on which Humanity has been swinging for eons and eons.

We stated our fist war in "Heaven." The result was the creation of our subconsciousness. It is the child of war. All those Laws, which worked constructively, were reversed in subconsciousness. We brought Laws, which were so constructive down into a very destructive condition. This was done through ignorance, impatience and pride. But we must pay for it. The Law of Cause and Effect never fails. This condition was brought into being not only in humans but also in animals, plants and in the elements. There were no carnivorous animals. Plants unfolded at their best. The elements created a beautiful climate. This was all changed.

When war started, it manifested first on a higher plane. It took quite a while for it to crystallize to this plane. We have now come to the modern age of awakening mind. Wars are worse than ever before. Peace has also unfolded. There is more desire for it than ever before. When the desire appears, the spirit of aggression gets the upper hand. We see this in every direction. When we try to conquer disease, more diseases appear more tenacious, more dangerous. Health seems to be in a downward condition. This is only temporary. Humans try to be more kind and more friendly, but this is upset by all the negative traits in subconsciousness. There is a continuous war between subconsciousness and Superconsciousness. The two opposing forces are fighting for dominion.

Which will win? When will the fight stop? No one knows when the end will come, but if we know the Laws of the Eternal, we can foresee that evil, in what ever form it appears, it will not have the last say, because it is a lie and a shadow by nature. The deeper the light becomes, the thinner the shadow. The apparent increase in the shadow is a delusion.

There is a continual struggle within us, between the Realm of Hades or subconsciousness and the Elysium Field where Love is the sole Ruler. We are waging a battle almost every moment of our lives. It is very important to realize the FourSquare in our daily battle. If one Corner of the Square is not balanced, the negative can enter and the battle is lost.

That was a wonderful promise of Peace and Good Will among men, but we will have to work for it. That goal of all mankind will have to be established. All the desires we have now for peace cannot stop the battle. There must be more than desire. Peace cannot remain inactive. It must become militant. When the spirit of peace will become understood by humans, it will become stronger because it will become a continuous fight. Peace should not be inactive. It must become dynamic. That is why humans, feeling this and not understanding it, make such statements as "We are fighting for peace. We are killing to win peace." In Korea, the United States is in a position where seemingly we are girding ourselves with the sword of justice to protect peace against an invader. We are losing because we are not fighting our own war. We are joining in a war for other people, a war that was none of our business. We have enough trouble in our own country to take all of our efforts. "Beware of foreign entanglements" were words of wisdom. This motto was first thrown overboard by President Woodrow Wilson. He destroyed the ambitions of Kaiser Wilhelm and helped Hitler to rise. In the second war we made the same mistake. We are trying to carry the torch for Humanity, but there is no fire in the torch. We have betrayed the motto, "In God We Trust" from A to Z. We are doomed to lose the Korean War. The consequences will be terrible. There is no use to attempt to make a peace treaty with an enemy who does not know the meaning of the word "Truth." There will be no successful negotiation of peace. What will happen? Probably revolution.

What shall we do? We are a small group who sincerely try to be on the side of peace. We are contributing to a cause, which will eventually win. We must live peace, be one with it. That is our problem, our final aim as Lightbearers. We must gird ourselves with the sword of courage. We must fight, not on the battlefield of killing, but on destroying all that is opposing real happiness within us. This is easier when we realize that we are not alone. We are fighting in the army of the Eternal. Invincible Hosts are at our side. It is the battle of the Eternal, with the Leader the Eternal Himself. When we realize this, there should be no fear in our hearts, no matter what the pressure of the negative or the Astral. We should not say we are alone. We are not. We should rise above it and say, "I have within me the Sword of Truth, my helmet is the Inspiration from above."

Lesson Thirty-Three

PROSAIC AND POETIC LIFE

In this very utilitarian and very prosaic age in which we live, people who are very intelligent disregard the poetic side of life. In reality it is very important. What does it mean to live a very prosaic life and to try to live a very poetic life? A prosaic life means to live a material, every day life. A poetic life lifts one above materiality into a Spiritual life.

As in every condition, the most desirable thing is to be between the two, where we have a fine foundation of stability. What we seek in life is stability. It means safety, and safety means a condition where we can grow and unfold in the best way. People think safety means an almost placid condition, safe without doing anything. People think if they are safe, they should not do anything. If we are safe, we should do the most. If we are safe, we can do things properly.

Some would say there is no adventure to this. This is a misconception. A true adventurer considers everything. He fist calculates everything he can. Then he says, "I will be able to meet those conditions which I cannot calculate." The whole of life is an adventure. To come to this physical plane is our greatest adventure. Adventurousness is a very wonderful spirit, a very wise spirit. It requires the use of our best mental qualities.

A balanced condition must be first developed within. The FourSquare Principle is the clearest definition of a balanced condition that we can have. Life cannot be all poetry. Life must take into consideration material things. The amount of money we have is not so important. Things are often easier with a small amount. More money requires greater judgment. One has to think out how the surplus, after immediate needs, can be used to the best advantage. What is left over is in one's hands by the operation of the Great Law. The Great Law says, "If you do not use it properly, you will be held responsible for it." You do not own life, life owns you. Money is not our money. It is the World's. We are only the trustees of it. Some day we will be called to account for all we use. There is a balance between being stingy and being generous, but generosity is one of the finest traits in our makeup.

Balance means harmony, and Harmony is the Kingdom of Heaven within. Jesus said, "Seek ye first the Kingdom of Heaven and everything else will be added unto you." The FourSquare is the best compass to the Kingdom of Heaven within, or Harmony or Balance.

A materialist tries to get out of life all of a material nature that he can. We should be a practical idealist or an idealistic materialist, both of which mean the same thing. Thus we give to God what belongs to God, and to Caesar, or Matter, what belongs to Caesar. In the present materialistic age, we have almost disregarded the poetic life. The fact that so much of the poetic side was taken out of children, left them with no incentive for anything beautiful in life. An incentive for beautiful things materially, mentally and Spiritually is an inner urge with which we are born. It must be manifested on the three planes. Within us is the natural incentive for everything beautiful and fine. This is poetry. Prosaic is matter of fact.

We are without knowing it, putting more poetry into life. Store displays, a few years ago, were very ordinary. Now there is an attempt to make them beautiful. A garland of flowers is often put around a pig in a window. Displays sometimes outdo the thing itself, which is again unbalance. Skyscrapers, which were first very plain and practical, are now being built more beautiful. Everything in Nature, which is practical, is also beautiful. Poetry is the sunshine that gilds everything it touches.

The general trend of literature is not toward immorality but unmorality. We are today in a state of unmorality. Materialism leads us more and more to unmorality. What we read has a tremendous influence on our life. That is why fairy tales, in olden days, were so appreciated by grownups as well as by children. Today, to read a fairy tale seems ridiculous. People think they are above it. In fairy tales there is a deep sense of morality, a Spiritual nature.

What can we do? The simple way is to get out of our system, the things which should not be there. Get rid of activities, which are wrong. If we are once determined that it will be removed, it will be so in time. There is within each of us the power to eliminate anything within us. We can never do it for another person, only for ourselves. A mental or emotional adjustment is easier if we first receive physical adjustment. Healing on the physical plane proves what can be done in a larger and deeper scale on the mental and emotion planes. If we do not appreciate healing on the physical plane, we will pay a heavy price for it.

Lesson Thirty-Four

SELF-RIGHTEOUSNESS

There is no such thing as Spiritual Pride. Pride shows lack of understanding. Those who think they have Spiritual Pride, cannot be loyal because they are loyal only to their own pride.

How could Spiritual Beings make the mistake we did, and Fall to this plane? The only satisfactory answer we can give, is that we did not know, and never will know, All. There is a continuous unfoldment. There was probably a loophole in our knowledge. The intense nature of a few, took advantage of this opening to express impatience. There was perhaps Spiritual Pride also. Probably the impatience to grasp everything all at once is why we made the mistake.

When we are very energetic physically, mentally and emotionally, we are usually very impatient. We are supposed to unfold gradually, and not by jerks. When things are done properly, every step has to be consolidated. When one is full of energy, he has the feeling that he would like to explode and suddenly grow big. This cannot be done.

In our desire to exceed the Law of natural unfoldment, we did just the opposite. This created a mental closing up which affected the whole of our physical aspect. We thus became Human Beings, by lowering our rate of vibration. This created our lower self, but did not affect our Higher Self. The same thing happens in a panic. The people rush towards an exit because they are impatient.

Human spiritual pride is our human ego which is so filled with its own sense of righteousness that its vision is beclouded.

If we understood the Fourth Dimension, we could use it. When we understand it, we will no longer be humans. If we understood it now, we would be able to dematerialize our bodies and pass through walls, and then rematerialize them. Our last test and last fight will be against our self-righteousness. The FourSquare Principle is so broad that It will always be right when applied to any activity. There is no self-righteousness in It. It is the Isness.

True tolerance is to forgive people because they do not know what is right. The mother lie is the personification of evil, or the devil.

Only a person with a three-dimensional mind can understand what righteousness is. When we get results by using the Laws, and we must always get results if the Laws are properly used, we should feel thankful, and not self-righteous. We should be thankful first to the Eternal, and then to the channel through which the Eternal was able to express.

We are so centered in our selves that we forget to be normal. We bury our own happiness. We should work out within ourselves, the qualities which will take us out of our present limitations. The moment the qualities are developed, in that moment the person will be lifted into something better.

Lesson Thirty-Five

SHARE SORROWS AND JOYS

There is a subject, which is of greatest importance to the Anglo-Saxon Race. These people, more than other Races, are introverts. They have repressed feelings. They do not like to share with others, things which are unpleasant. This sounds very logical, not to burden others with our troubles, but it is not logical.

For thousands of years it was accepted by Humanity that shared joy and shared sorrow is natural and human.

Both introverts and extroverts are not normal. We should always follow the middle road. We should use judgment when and with whom we share joy and sorrows.

The reason Anglo-Saxons keep sorrows to themselves is, first, they want to be very manly. They are afraid of being called a sissy. Second, they do not want to burden those who they love with their troubles.

Real love is based on help and consideration. There is no greater joy for Love, than to give. The Eternal Father was first a Giver. This is also seen in Nature. We should be givers. This awakens a corresponding return. We rob our friends of the joy of comforting us. This is unnatural and abnormal. Shared joy is double joy, and shared sorrow is half a sorrow. Friendship is the most sacred feeling a person can have.

Lesson Thirty-Six

SILENCE IS GOLDEN

There is a saying that speech is silver but Silence is golden. We know from practical experience and from what we see in others, both on a small scale and on a large scale, the power of speech. People are affected, masses swayed and world events changed. We are familiar with the verse—"In the beginning was the Word, and the Word was with God, and the Word was God." Translating this, we have, In the beginning was Power and the Power was with God and the Power was God. Also it is said say to the mountain, "Cast thyself into the sea and it will be so." We also know in legends, that a magic word could achieve a miracle. A word is more powerful than a thought because we are living on the material plane.

A thought must be manifest, and the easiest manifestation is the word. It is not the only manifestation. Some people can see thoughts, as thought forms. Those who see ghosts are usually only seeing the thought form of a departed being whom they are thinking about. However, a thought translated into a sound is more satisfactory. It is a power. This power can be used for good or evil. Some of the most beautiful things that have come to Humanity have been imported by words. The voice of the speaker must be harmonious to the words spoken. Otherwise, it is like a scratchy needle on a beautiful record. That is why people should cultivate their voices. We do not like to listen to the cawing of a crow. People want to sing, but they have not learned to modulate their words in talking. In the present condition of the World, we have gone so far in the wrong direction that we do not recognize a good voice.

Speech has been given to us for the expression of our feelings. All Nature has speech. All animals, birds, plants speak with each other, but we cannot understand them. Those old ideas that some people can understand animals are based on facts. Animal trainers, who really love their animals, learn to talk with them and understand them. I have often tried to perceive what trees say to each other or to me.

Speech has a direct connection with Truth. Animals talking to each other never lie. If you ever lie to an animal, he will never trust you again, because animals perceive the Truth. We should never slip from the straight meaning of what we intend to say. What we think, we should say, and what we say, we should think.

Speech is very precious. It is the silver gate through which we enter this World. When we walk through the gate of silver, we achieve what is right. When we walk through a gate that is adulterated, we achieve that which is wrong. Silver represents the spoken word. Gold is silence. There is much more silver in this World that gold.

The diamond today is the most precious stone. If there were tons of them, people would not want them. When there are abundant crops, the prices go down. When there is a scarcity, the prices go up. If gold would be as abundant as silver, it would be of the same value. At the present time, we have billions and billions of dollars worth of gold taken out of circulation and stored at Fort Knox, Kentucky. Those directing the destinies of this country have removed Silence from circulation. That indicates the beginning of decay. Gold has never been used for destruction. Silver has been used.

The spoken word and silence should go hand in hand. In speeches, words should be followed by some silence. Humans do not understand this. One should understand it to be a proper leader, either of a small shop or a big country. We should use with discrimination the spoken word and silence. If we are too silent, we are unbalanced. People are annoyed by too much talking, but they do not mind a silent person. Silence is greater than speech. Silence in words does not mean silence in thoughts. There never can be complete stoppage of thinking. Even in our dreams, we think. Silence is the background of thinking. And individual life can be completely changed by thinking, but not by talking.

True friendship is measured by the amount of silence. They can commune the best by Silence. Superconsciousness is the still small voice, which speaks only in silence. In silence we can commune with our Higher Self and with God.

Lesson Thirty-Seven

SOLUTIONS OF PROBLEMS IN SLEEP

A problem solved in our sleep, is solved by our Higher Self, and not by our subconsciousness. The solution of a problem means harmonization, which leads to a satisfactory answer.

All writers on mind base their conclusions on the power which subconsciousness has to multiply. The power of multiplication is everywhere around us, but the power of subconsciousness does not mean that it is correct multiplication. We cannot deny to subconsciousness the power of multiplication, but we must come to the conclusion that those multiplications are not correct. Subconsciousness cannot use its own power in a correct way; therefore any answers from it, cannot be right.

Investigators believe there is unlimited power in subconsciousness; therefore they think we can find the solution of all problems in it. Investigators do not approach the power from the FourSquare Principle, but on the triangle, omitting the power of mind. Physicists do not credit Supreme Intelligence with intelligence, and are therefore atheists. THE LIGHTBEARERS state that subconsciousness has no intelligence, but has instead chaos. Subconsciousness understands orders. Therefore we can order it, when going to sleep, to awaken us at a certain hour, and it will obey the order. We can also rely on our Higher Self to awaken us at a certain hours, and It will do so.

Lesson Thirty-Eight

STRENGTH

The assertion of Right in the face of Wrong makes us that much stronger. In the face of misstatements or danger, if we assert ourselves we grow stronger.

We cannot succeed in the direction of Wisdom, Truth, Law and Harmony unless we grow stronger. These characteristics, if not backed by Energy, have no effect at all. Nature first put Energy in Her pattern. Without it, Nature would fail.

Buddha and Jesus, who emphasized Love, both stressed strong Love, burning Love. Unfortunately through all the centuries the very spirit of those Teachings has not been understood.

People confuse strength with brutality. Real strength is not brutal, because it is conscious of its own power. Brutality shows an inferiority complex. Such people have to prove to themselves that they are strong. Brutality is therefore a weakness.

Real strength is gentle yet unbelievably strong. Consider the ocean, how gentle is its water, so smooth, and yet so powerful. Consider the wind, the gentle breeze, yet how strong it can be. Consider the diamond. It is the strongest stone we know. Its powder is the finest powder, yet it can polish the hardest material. It is the same way with people. The strongest human character can handle itself.

Because strength is a Spiritual quality, we have to develop it. Because of this we are given many opportunities to do so. These are tests. In primitive times the physical had the greatest tests. It required determination on the mental plane and stimulation on the physical plane.

In the face of present day conditions, where we find weakness on the physical, mental and emotional planes, the more Humanity disintegrates the more we should work in the opposite direction. We should not accept weakness. Never submit to anything wrong. It does not pay.

The Great Law will not lead us to a point and then drop us. That is the negative. If we do not give in, we are always able, in some way, to accomplish.

Each time we mentally protest and succeed, we gain in Spiritual strength. It is the quality of strength and not the quantity that counts. This is not what the World is living and teaching now, but it is the only true way.

This is a very important matter. On our Spiritual strength will depend not only our own success, but the welfare of Humanity. As long as Humanity will exist, strength will be first, because it is the first thing in creation.

Lesson Thirty-Nine

THE FOUR SEASONS

We are going to analyze tonight something which we all know very well, but which has so many aspects which are not well known and understood. I want to discuss tonight about the four seasons or the year: the Spring, the Summer, Fall and the Winter.

Those seasons are more definitely outlined in what we call the Temperate Zone. In the cold regions, though they are also present, they are not so well balanced as they are in the Temperate Zone, and neither are they in the so-called Tropics. The Temperate Zone seems to be like a standard climate. It is between the two opposites, the two extremes: extreme heat and extreme cold, and that is why the Temperate Zone is considered probably the healthiest climate for anyone to live in, produces stronger people both physically and mentally – the zone where everything has a chance to unfold itself at its best. That Temperate Zone because of its advantages is symbolic to us of the Golden Rule between the two extremes.

So let's analyze, therefore, those four seasons as they come and go in the Temperate Zone. We have first the season called spring. Now the Spring is the season where everything seems to be born, awakened. It is the so-called Awakening of Nature. It is the season when things are planted and where everything starts from the winter season with their lovely green color as background for many other colors. Green is the color of Hope. Green, as you know from scientific investigations, is really condensed sunshine, because the green color of the leaves, chlorophyll, is condensed sunshine, and when the spring comes it is also the season of hopes, of joy, of everything the best which is manifested not only around us but in us. It is the Season of Youth.

In a way, it is the most important season of all season, because it is the season, which determines the rest of our life. If we live that spring of our life properly, the rest of our life will be accordingly. The birds sing, build their nests – they mate, they start training their children. The earth is covered with flowers, the trees with blossoms – it is a regular holiday attire for the whole of Nature. Life is on parade, and then comes the Summer, where everything that started in the Spring unfolds, grows, increases in every direction in strength and in beauty – the season where the noon of Life seems to be reached. The little birds, which were fledglings in the Spring, have grown their wings, can fly and can live a life of their own. The trees, which bore the promise of fruition, start the fruits, the flowers become seeds. New summer flowers start. It is a season of richness – as I said, the Noon of Life.

And then comes the Fall, the season when everything, which we have started in the Spring and cultivated throughout the Summer, comes to fruition. The fields turn yellow; the trees, also. There is a sweetness in the air, something mellow – the sweetness of evening, twilight, that beautiful combination of light and the coming darkness. It is a rich season, too, because everything which was done in the Spring and in the Summer is now to be gathered in the Fall, to be enjoyed, to be then stored for the coming winter and to be used for the following Spring. It is a season where we look upon the past and if the past lived up to our expectations and we lived up to the expectations the previous seasons presented to us, the result is pleasing and we say to ourselves, It was well done. It is a season where for the last time, so to speak, strength of every kind is put to task to perform its last duties for the coming Winter.

And then comes the Winter, the Season of Rest. Snow covers the fields, protects the roots from excessive cold, and Nature seems to have gone asleep – but it hasn't gone asleep. It is a time when all the trophies which were gathered together in the Fall, are, so to speak, properly distributed to be used for the coming spring. It is a season where rest in soft, gentle activities is the keynote.

Those are the seasons as they come and go on this earth in the temperate climate, and usually, as you all know, they are divided on this earth into four – three months in each season, according, naturally to the movement of the earth around the Sun. Well, those seasons started when the earth started to rotate around the Sun, or rather revolve around the Sun, and those seasons will come and go until the earth's rotation around the sun will slow down and come to an end.

Those seasons are the seasons also of our lives – they are more than symbolic. Each season stands for a certain period of our life. We are born in the season of Spring and because it is like the awakening to a new day, everything seems so bright, so interesting to us. We sing because the world sings, Nature sings, birds sing – everything is happiness. It is a season, as I said, where we for the first time as children begin to love our parents, then those who are around us and those who become later on our life companions.

The love of that first season remains throughout the whole of our life as an outstanding feature, as it is a season which impresses us more than any other season, because we are like wax. Our hearts and our minds are pliable and therefore we take in everything with so much more enthusiasm; it is also the season of Enthusiasm.

Beautiful as that season is, Nature teaches us that it isn't only a season of enjoyment. It is a season which is extraordinarily well balanced between working constructively, unfolding our own self, and enjoying our own work, our own unfoldment. When the birds build their nest, they sing. When the flowers bloom, they send out fragrance. Everything in Nature both works and enjoys the work. Unfortunately, we human beings have not understood the great deep lesson the Spring wants us to learn. So many people think that the Spring is nothing but the season of enjoyment without work, because they do not realize that work is also enjoyment. It is quite obvious that a plant or a tree during the springtime when the warm rays dry the moisture of the earth, its roots work harder than ever after the winter sleep to gather as much as they can of the water to feed themselves. Birds when they are building their nests enjoy that work, because they know they need a room for the future family, and when the little fledglings are hatched out of their eggs, both parents work hard to provide the food for those fledglings – but they sing also at the same time. All that work is done with joy, with love, and the little ones are brought up in love.

But the parents watch that when they have grown up they should learn the ways of life, that they should also learn, in their turn, how to find their own food, how to provide for themselves, how to fly, how to gain their ends, how to discriminate between a friend and an enemy, how to take the proper food and leave that which is not right because it is not digestible.

All those lessons are taught by all the animals and they are taught with the assurance that they will be proper and they usually are, and so throughout the millions and millions of years every animal, every bird, every tree and every plant continues the life of its species with songs and joy. We were meant to do the same thing, because life was not meant to be such a hardship as life is today for most of us. In spite of our becoming human beings, which we were not intended to be because it was a lowering of our rate of vibration which out of free spirits made us limited mortals, Mother Nature in her graciousness said to herself, "Even if they have forsaken me, even if they have forgotten my Laws, I am still the Mother and I still will look after them, and I will still be gracious to them." And that is why Mother Nature provided that beautiful spring for us to take advantage of and to enjoy, and the same with Summer.

But what have most human beings done with the spring of their life? As I said before, they thought that the Spring is only there to have fun and no hopes, so to speak, for a better and I would say broader unfoldment of life, no responsibilities – just fun. Well, all right, as long as they are young, as long as the spring of life is there, that seems to them to be the right thing to do. But then comes the Summer, which is an unfoldment of the Spring – more strength, more responsibilities, bigger outlook on Life, bigger demand from life, and bigger, so to speak, of everything. That which has not been started in the Spring must be sowed in the Summer and that which has been neglected in the Spring must be taken care of in the Summer, and though it may be started in the Summer, remember, there is that much shorter time to grow.

Though it is quite true that it is never too late to do the right thing, even at the eleventh hour, usually everything, which we do, demands some time to mature, to grow, to ripen. Before it ripens to the proper stature, size, and especially according to the bigness of the problem, you must give that much more time for those problems to grow, and those who have neglected to do the right thing during the Spring probably will continue to neglect it during the Summer, because the summer of their lives is still a very alluring season. They feel still young, they feel stronger than ever before, with maybe more demands from life, yet at the same time with less willingness to give more to Life. And they think that the Summer will endure forever, just like those who lived through the Spring always thought that the Spring will endure forever, and without noticing, out of the Spring they slipped into Summer, and sometimes they are living the Summer believing that it is still Spring, not the Summer, and that that will last forever. But it does not. There comes a time when the Fall knocks at the door and says, "Now let's see what you have done during the Summer and during the Spring. What have you gathered together? You received the talents at your birth in the Spring – what have you done with those talents? Show your hand."

And those who have done something with their talents, they are there to give the answer in the Fall: "Here, we have done things" and the Fall tells them, "Go harvest it." If you worked in the field, that is your harvest. If you worked in the orchard, that is your harvest. If you worked in any other department of life you will find your harvest waiting for you, that the Fall has matured everything into fruition. If you planted a good seed, you will reap a good harvest. If you planted a bad seed, you will reap a bad harvest, and if you didn't plant any seed, your hands will be empty.

Now that is the season of the year which for the people who used the previous two seasons properly, gives probably the greatest satisfaction. They are still strong enough in body and mind to enjoy the fruits of their work. They have learned through experience all the various lessons which the precious seasons have taught them. They have seen their children grow into men and women and in their turn probably having their children, too. They have gained rest combined with the love of their own, and there they stand, so to speak, in the soft evening, in the twilight, where everything is so mellow and so are their characteristics – strong and yet mellow, and they look toward the last season, the Winter.

And then comes the Winter of their life, the winter which is for everyone, rest. The fruits which they gathered in the Fall of every kind, be they material, mental or emotional fruits, they are now to enjoy that, not to work any more. The gathering has taken place in the Fall – nobody gathers in the Winter – and is stored for the Winter season, to be used during the Winter. It is a season of a lovely quiet and peace. It prepares for another life, for another awakening, maybe in another world, and they are looking forward, those who have gone through the precious three seasons the way they could and should, to that life. They are serenely passing through the season of the Winter of their life where the snow covers their heads, just like it covers the ground and the trees, and they are lovely, too, in their own way. Lovely with that serenity of a peace which is not any more of the earthly kind. They wait for the new day for them to come.

That is how those who lived the four seasons properly face life. But for those who have not lived properly, see what the winter brings to them. Empty handed already in the fall, they are depending on charity, facing want and poverty, limitation of body and mind in every direction, depleted in body and mind, because they did not live and take advantage of all that the previous seasons had to offer them. That winter for them then is misery. Instead of being maybe so lovely and quiet a winter, it is just a cold, frosty season – no gentleness, but cold. No protection as a soft snow, but the winds of unhappiness even blowing away the little protection the snow gives.

The gentleness of the Winter season; that is what the snow symbolizes. They have nothing but bitter cold there, and they can only say, "When will that cold stop? When will that Winter come to an end?" and they count those days. Those who have shaped their lives properly into the proper winter can live their lives serenely. For those who have not done that every moment is a torture and they do not enjoy their last stay on earth the way they could enjoy it.

Whose fault is all this? It is the fault of Humanity. Humanity has not been taught to make use of their own qualities according to their season. They have wasted their lives without taking advantage of the countless opportunities, which the seasons were bringing to them. That is why life is not such a simple problem. That is why life has to be understood. That is why life when understood can, in spite of all the difficulties we have to overcome, become a beautiful life, each season bringing the joys of that season.

Now these are the Four Seasons throughout the human life, but then remember those Four Seasons are not only passing through the whole of human life. Human life is not only divided into four according to the Four Seasons. The Four Seasons are continually there present every moment of our life, every day of our life. You may say, How? That is simple to understand. Whatever we do, whatever we feel, whatever we think is a unit, which has its Four Seasons. It starts – it is the Spring; it grows – it is the Summer; it becomes in full fruition – it is the Fall, and it is to be enjoyed, to be taken advantage of in the Winter.

Well now remember that in those seasons, like in everything else in Life, the Law of Cause and Effect plays a continual and fundamental role. The Spring is the cause; Winter is the final effect, and for that very reason whatever we do we should always try to do it according to the FourSquare, because the FourSquare in our life is not only our guide, but is our inspiration. It is the way we measure and divide our life in the proper way. Remember, the whole of our life is Number 12 – three multiplied by four. Each corner has it three-dimensional aspect: the length, the width and the depth, and therefore every action has its three-dimensional aspect, too – every thought the same, every feeling the same – and it has also accordingly and correspondingly the Four Seasons.

Whenever we start a thought, it should be naturally a constructive thought to start with, full of energy, full of enthusiasm. Again I emphasize it should be the right kind of thought, and then we should cultivate that thought, make it pass through the season of the Summer to the point where it becomes something real, something which we can put into practice, use, and when it has grown to that extent, then we embody that thought, bury that thought into a material expression, be it a word, be it an act. That is the winter of the thought, but that is also the Spring of the act. The winter of the thought culminating in the act starts the spring of the act, and there the same starts again. The thought implanted in the act blossoms forth in the act in full vigor, and that is the spring of the act. And then we have to nurse that Spring into the Summer; nurse that act to make it grow so as to have its full fruition in the Fall. And when we have it in full fruition in the Fall, then we gather it together – the results of our act, of our manifestations in a bodily form – and then we are to enjoy it as long as it lasts.

Now there, therefore, we have that great measurement of the whole of our life in Four Seasons so divided into every moment of our human life and sub-divided according to the three planes; the plane of the emotions, the plane of the thought and the plane of the material expressions.

Now when we understand all this, see how differently we can live our lives and how interesting our life will become when lived that way. But how few know how to do it and how still less in numbers are those who are doing it.

Remember also this, that as in one year the seasons never repeat themselves, so in one incarnation the seasons never repeat themselves. And in one thought the seasons never repeat themselves, in one action, in one feeling, the seasons never repeat themselves – for them it is finished. A new one may start, yes, but for that one it is finished. Each thought, each feeling, each action has its definite appointed time for the Four Seasons to give, and when they are manifested, that is a closed chapter. That is because of the Law of Cause and Effect. Once the cause culminates in an effect, that chapter is finished. Another cause may start to terminate in another thing; but the same one never does.

Now this is a most important thing, because how often if we do not live our life as intelligently as we could and should, we say to our own self: "If I could only turn back the hands of Time, if I could relive." It is impossible. Even if we try to relive a thing, it can't be done, for the very simple reason because we change all the time, we are never the same two moment in our life, and though we would like to relive, to live again that which we think we could have lived better, the moment we try we cannot succeed, because we are not the same people, not the same beings we were when we lived those moments, and to be again the same people is impossible, because that would be against the Law of Evolution, it would be against progress. It would be just like a butterfly turning back into a caterpillar – it can't be done, and for that very reason whenever there is an opportunity in life we should always try to make the best use of that opportunity, for the simple reason that the same opportunity never come to us again. We can have similar opportunities, we can sometimes make opportunities, create opportunities, but still they are different opportunities.

And that is also a very important lesson to learn, because the seasons of our life are different units of life, and each opportunity carries within itself the different seasons, they are indissolubly connected one with another. And in the Spring there is the opportunity to create; in the Summer there is opportunity to increase the creation; in the Fall there is opportunity to gather the creation, and in the Winter is the opportunity to spend properly that, which has been gathered.

Now this is Life and how lovely and how interesting it is according to the Four Seasons, but again, as I said before, who understands that? Few.

And see how those Four Seasons are intimately connected with the FourSquare. The season of the Spring is the corner of Energy; the season of the summer is the corner of Wisdom, of Mind; the season of the Fall is the corner of Law, of Truth – it is all genuine and true, and the truth is revealed. If a man achieved something, if he has done something right in the Fall, it is revealed that he has done the right thing. If he has done something wrong in the Fall at the moment of fruition it is shown that he did the wrong thing.

The Fall is a very important part of our human life, as in the Seasons it is the Day of Judgment. What happens if the Day of Judgment, so to speak, is the Winter? We then in the winter enjoy or suffer according to what we gathered or missed during the previous season. There as in the Day of Judgment to speak symbolically, is everybody to be weighed in the balance. In the Fall we balance everything, it is literally that way – how much of the right, how much of the wrong. So you see, when people speak of the Day of Judgment they think of something entirely different, and they do not realize that every day in every field of our human activities the Day of Judgment takes place, and usually it is our own conscience, which is our judge.

If people would understand how life goes on much more within us than it does outside of us – I do not mean that we live more an inner life than an outer life, in an harmonious condition the two ought to be balanced. The inner life should not exceed the outer life, neither should the outer life exceed the inner life; but it is always better to have a richer inner life than a richer outer life, because the inner life provides the material for the outer life, and the outer life without the inner life is like a tree without fruits. It is like a flower which is cut off the bush, it will endure for only a certain length of time.

Now people do not realize that. We think so much of that outer life. As I say, it has its value, but its permanency, its richness, is all dependent on the inner life. That is why we have that advantage that if we cultivate our inner life properly and continually manifest in our outer expression as much as we live within we will never be poor without. We may pass through some hard moments due maybe to some mistakes, maybe due to some test we have to go though in order to find our own self, to find out how strong we are, how well we can face conditions which are not so good – anybody can face good conditions, that does not require any strength. Strength is only needed when things do not work out so good, but we with that inner strength, which is called symbolically the Kingdom of Harmony within, with that Kingdom of Harmony within we can always supply the harmony without, because the harmony within is the cause of the harmony without. That is why we should always try to concentrate all our efforts to start the proper cause, or rather to start the cause properly. And how do we start the cause properly; By letting it go through all the Four Seasons.

Now see the advantage of those Four Seasons. There in the Law of Cause and Effect we have the Four Seasons in one – why? Because the Law of Cause and Effect does not belong only to the three-dimensional world; it belongs to the Fourth Dimension. It belongs to the world where time and space are no more, where there is Eternity and Infinity – to the dimension, which surrounds us. Every part of us is surrounded by that, physically, mentally and emotionally, and in that fourth-dimensional world, cause and effect are one. Spring, summer, fall and winter are one, because they are a year with no division. In the Fourth Dimension, there is no, so to speak, human concept of divisions.

The Fourth Dimension, representing the FourSquare, unites everything in the FourSquare. There Life, Mind, Truth and Love all unite and you cannot separate them, because it would not be the FourSquare – in the FourSquare everything is united and that is why it is one. They are, so to speak, instantaneous and simultaneous, though according to a certain logical order, and that is why when we understand Life, all those thoughts, all those feelings, all those deeds which do become fourth-dimensional deeds, they become things beyond the human concept of Life. They bring us and hold us in that harmonious condition of the FourSquare. The more we live it, the closer we come to a realization of our oneness with that FourSquare, and the more we are benefited by the qualities of the FourSquare. More energy, more wisdom, more honesty, sincerity and more enjoyment and happiness. It is all, you see, connected. Life is one; all seasons are one. They do not extend themselves as we see in life through those four long periods. Even in our earthly life, when we have lived them through, when we are ready to step into another condition, they are to us just a moment we have lived through and yet they were the four long seasons of our earthly journey, where we started as a child and finished as old men and women.

Now in our present condition of life probably it is more difficult than ever before to live those four seasons as they should be lived, because of the strange attitude of youth toward Old Age. In days gone by old age was respected, in most cases, and people were taught to honor those who have reached a certain limit of their earthly life because of their experience and sometimes wisdom. Today Youth says: "The world is mine. To me alone is that world to be served. To me it is given."

The world is not given to one season. The world belongs to the four seasons, they come and go. The young men have their place in life; so have mature people; so have the middle-aged people; so have the old, and they all occupy a certain place, certain corners in the FourSquare of Life, and each corner should be working in harmony with the other corners. It is the corner of old age, which faces the corner of maturity. There in maturity should people begin to look toward the day when they will be old, because the fourth corner is the corner of Winter, and the Mind corner is the second corner.

People to some extent think of their security for old age when they have reached maturity, begin to take care of it, but that is not enough. Material security is not sufficient. We want more than a roof over our heads and the walls surrounding us. We want windows through which we can look at the world and enjoy, and we want the fresh air entering through those windows. We want a door in that house so as to be able to step out and bask ourselves in the sunshine. Those things are more important in a way than security. One is secure in a prison cell, but one is not only secure – one is imprisoned in that security, and that is what so many people do not understand. They provide for themselves what we may call material security, but that is all. They build around themselves a prison cell and remain and remain during their old age in those prison cells instead of enjoying life outside of them. Better a little hole with windows and doors and no bars, no chains.

Now that security is only achieved when we have lived our life according to the seasons. You remember that in our Commandment it says, "Thus living can you only build to freedom, strength and happiness in Life." We start building for freedom in the spring, and we enjoy the freedom, which we have built, in the winter.

Think, for instance, how most human beings when they are getting old instead of being broadminded, instead of having the freedom which their experience and the many years they have lived have developed in them, how limited they are, how crystallized. They are not living. They are dead stone, yet they should be like a free wind. The wind does not grow old. Remember the wind blows as well in the winter as it does in the spring – people forget that. And if Old Age would have lived up to its own problem, would carry it out, probably the Youth of today would look up to Old Age differently. We cannot blame only Youth for taking that attitude toward the older people. If the old people are sometimes regarded as old fogies, sometimes old fools, there must be a reason for it, because with the little knowledge and understanding that Youth has—for they cannot have much of it, you can have everything in Youth except experience – they don't have experience, but because they have intelligence, they can judge if other people have had experience, because experience is noticeable. It is, so to speak, like the outside appearance of somebody, like a man who knows how to dress himself. He will have the experience to dress himself properly. The same with a woman, and you admit it, say, "Well, they have the experience." The way we act, the way we think, the way we talk, all show the experience we have had and if we talk in the right way and if we act in the right way, and especially if we think in the right way, that will be noticeable, and we would have then the liking of Youth, because Youth is always willing to learn something from the people whom they think could teach them. Youth has that insatiable desire to know, to improve – most of them, even those who are, so to speak, idling away their lives, still want something even in their search for idle dreams. It is that desire, that spirit of adventure, of Youth, and if they can find an inspiration in Old Age which can tell them of their own efforts, or their own experience, or their own achievements, it would be a wonderful life on earth. But I must say, as I belong to the old generation, that the old generation failed the young one and the young one, naturally, is failing the old generation. But the fault is not with the young generation though it seems to be. The fault is with the old generation. They have not shown themselves as the proper example. In other words, they have destroyed within the young generation the ideals that had to start with; they disappointed the ones who expected so much – and then what? We have life as life is today.

But that does not mean because life is the way it is today that we in our individual lives should follow the example of other people. Remember, each one of us, we are to live our own life the best we know, and if we live it according to the principles we have so clearly and so simply outlined in our FourSquare Teachings, we will always fit in with the lives of other people who try to live the same, and if we do not fit in, we should not worry at all, because remember, it is like this: If we are FourSquare, we are adamant, nothing can break through that FourSquare. Nothing can, so to speak, dispose of our corners, because they are in the Eternal and anything, which tries to jeopardize, to combat that condition, to mangle it, can never mangle it, but will be mangled themselves. It is just like an ordinary piece of weak clay trying to break through a diamond. The clay no matter how hard it is, will be broken by the diamond – and that is what we should remember in life. If we are like the FourSquare, we are like a diamond and we cannot be broken by outside influences and conditions, but we will break the outside influence condition because they are not FourSquare – they are Clay. If they are still soft clay which has not hardened, they will take the form of our FourSquare. If they are hardened and dry where they cannot any more show their elasticity, it will just break them, they will crumble into dust.

Now that is what we ought to remember and yet we are always trying to adjust the diamond conditions of our FourSquare to the clay condition of the world. Why should we? It doesn't pay. We lose and the world does not gain, because remember, if that which is clay which is dust, in contacting us turns to dust, the sooner it turns to dust, the better it is, because it leaves space and time for something better to take its place. You see, we should in our life use more wisdom that we do. Wisdom and emotion should be balanced and we should not let emotion overbalance us. We should not try to adjust ourselves to others beyond the limits of our own, so to speak, FourSquare. If we would always bear that in mind, probably we would never make any mistakes, for we would be growing in strength and in stature in every way, and we would live the seasons of our life FourSquare. Each season FourSquare and the Four Seasons FourSquare, too. In order to have a FourSquare year, we have to live the seasons FoursSquare, and not just one season Foursquare, not start living in a FourSquare kind of way, like in the Spring, and then become negligent and not persevere, not so to speak, take care of that which we have started and then when we have reached the Fall say "Well, what do I care what I have gathered or I didn't gather myself?" I can gather through somebody else, in somebody else's orchards. So many people try to reap what they have not sown, go into somebody else's orchard and pluck the fruits, which they have not planted, or at least taken care of. That is what usually people do and they think they can get away with it. We never can. We can perhaps for a season, for a time, but that time is comparatively very short. In other words, only the right attitude in life, only the right thought, the right feeling, the right action, is to be considered, because they are the only ones, which are unbreakable – they are adamant.

Now that is all for tonight and if you have some questions to ask, you may ask me.

Seasons should be balanced, but as you say, in life seasons sometimes outbalance each other. According to the calendar, according to the movement of the earth around the sun, they are all balanced – balanced to the minute; therefore, according to the Law and the demand of the principle of Harmony they should be balanced, but very often they become unbalanced, like we say that with some people Spring is perennial. You see very often people when they have reached a very mature age still want to be like spring chickens. Well, it never works. They would like to, but they can't – and to want to but can't, is a very pitiful sight.

Now remember, that does not mean that when one has reached even the Winter season one should be just like, well, dust. Remember, the snow can become very brilliant when the sun shines and when the sun sets it has lovely tints, and in the moonlight it glitters like diamonds. Therefore, even in the winter we can reflect all the beauty, but in a different way. Now that is what human beings should understand. That is what the wise men and women of days gone by did understand and that is what is rather difficult now for the present. Today people do not understand and there is a reason for it. Things like that do not happen without a reason, and the reason is not a superficial one; it is very deep.

People more and more realize that there is no Old Age that they are moving into a climate like semi-tropic where there is no winter, which is, if you like, I would not say a step in advance or improvement, but which is gentler and more alluring than the temperate climate – the semi-tropic.

Now in the semi-tropic climate, as I just stated, the seasons are not so clearly outlined though they are there and the Winter there is not the Winter of the, well, temperate zone. And people more and more now move out of the temperate zone, figuratively speaking, mentally into a semi-tropic condition of mind where they do not want to recognize Old Age.

Now we could call the Realm of Harmony a semi-tropic condition where everything is most exuberant, without excessive heart and without, naturally, cold. It is like an Eternal Spring. Now probably life in the Realm of Harmony is like an Eternal Spring, but it isn't an Eternal Spring. It is spring, summer, fall and winter, which have each a little distinction; though each one has its proper function, they function as one in the proper way. There is also the time of planting, the time of cultivating, the time of maturing and the time of rest, like in the temperate zone, only it is not so obvious.

Now in the condition probably of Harmony there would be like a semi-tropic condition of our mind where we would never grow old and yet continually pass through the Season of Spring, of Summer, of the Fall and of the Winter without growing old and without dying. Now this is probably more and more dawning upon Humanity and that is why Humanity today, especially through women who are more intuitive than men, feels that Old Age should not be. There should be advanced years, but not Old Age; it should be an ageless condition which is a perpetual noon at its height, and that naturally has a tremendous influence on the whole of the life of people.

Now with scientists more and more bringing to humanity the assurance that we are only living half of our life; that while three score and ten, the Biblical limit, is a long limit, it is only half of the limit that we should live to about 150 years. In other words, a man and woman of 75 should be at their height – they should be like a woman of 35 or a man or 35 is now.

Well, as I say, human beings begin to feel that and that is why there is the saying, "Life begins at 80." Sometimes it is a rather funny combination – a man feels young and acts young and looks old, and when he looks old and feels young and acts young, he looks foolish, because certain ways correspond to certain periods of life. But those things by and by probably will be modified, will be adjusted, and at least there is that consolation that more and more human beings refuse to accept Old Age.

In days gone by they grew old gracefully, which was a very lovely thing, and it is still very lovely to grow old gracefully, for each one can grow old and maintain to some extent one's vigor of body and mind and of emotion. That is a very lovely thing, but it should be modified. We are after all still on this earth and the demands of life on earth are to be given some consideration. But, in any case, they seek expression in cities where people are much more progressive than in the county. There are all those beauty parlors, which help women, and men, to fight, well, advancing Old Age by counter-attacks.

Well, it is interesting and you can't help it, it is there and there must be a reason for it, and as I say, there must be a much deeper reason than appears on the surface, because remember, the Soul is perennial. The Soul, after all, refuses to be considered as growing old; it is only our human mind. It is the human mind, which grows old, and not the human Soul, and there comes the conflict between the Soul and the human mind. The Soul says, I am still young, and the mind says, how about your arthritis and what about you double chin and what about your gray hair and what about this and that? And the mind by and by usually wins the battle, but the Soul should not give up to win the battle. You see, that is what I am battling for. The doctor said, "Put on glasses." Well, I don't mind to have glasses, but to go around all day long with those kind of contraptions sitting on your nose and looking like through a gold fish bowl at the walls of the world – well, I don't think that is interesting and I have been fighting that all the time. If it were not for that I would be wearing glasses and be more, well, less comfortable with glasses, and ignorant people would say, "Well, isn't he looking wise, like a professor. One pair of eyes is not enough, he has two pairs"

Well, was the answer satisfactory?

Lesson Forty

THE SPHERE

When we put our hands together to form The Sphere, it is like holding the Light. This is seen in the picture of The Morning Star. This was not definitely planned. I unconsciously held my hands this way while posing, and did not notice it until I saw the painting. The Flame was intended to be a Light, but the artist saw it as a Star and painted it that way. She said, that as she looked at the Flame, it changed to the appearance of a Star. We thus have a painting of the Messenger carrying in the Sphere, a Star, the Morning Star.

When we make The Sphere, we have concentrated Light. Inside The Sphere is a rotary movement. The longer we hold The Sphere, the stronger the rotary movement becomes. Included in The Sphere is the Six-Pointed Star of Power, Abundance, Wisdom, Law, Harmony, Protection.

The Sphere stimulates the Spiritual Self of the person whom we place in It. His stimulated Spiritual Self in turn stimulates his Life Center, and brings about a healing. After placing the person in The Sphere, we should think of Harmony. The realization of Harmony is not easy. We should just try to feel It.

There is the question whether one should place his own Spiritual Self in The Sphere in addition to that of the patient. The advantage is that one becomes more closely in contact with the patient. In doing so, place first oneself, saying, "I am in The Sphere," then the name of the patient or problem. The disadvantage is that if one has not contacted the Eternal Power, one may take on the sickness temporarily of the patient. A good healer is usually successful in protecting himself from this.

The Sphere is the maximum concentration of Power so far known to us, provided we are in contact with the Eternal Power. If we are not in contact, The Sphere is only a concentration of human power, and anything negative can enter It.

Lesson Forty-One

THE STORY OF THE MATCH

There was a time in the life of the match, when the match was not a match. It was part of a big tree, a cottonwood tree. The tree grew in a beautiful forest. There was no worry, because the tree took care of itself. Those were wonderful days. The sun shone, the rain watered the ground. Everything was so prosperous, so peaceful, so harmonious.

Then something happened within the trunk of the tree. There seemed to be a feeling of revolt. The individual parts felt tied to the tree, felt that they had no freedom. They wanted to be free. More and more, within the tree, the individual parts started growing. They felt they wanted to do by themselves the thing, which they wanted to do.

As in Heaven, all desire comes true. An axman came and cut down the tree, and took it to a mill, and cut it up. Looking at some of the wood, the owners said, that is no good, it is too soft, we will burn it up. A man with more vision said, we may burn it but in a different way. We will make matches of it. Those individual parts of the tree became wood for matches. When the wood for the little match was cut, it said, "Now I am free. I will go into the World and do as I want to do."

But it was not free. The end of it had to be put in phosphorous solution. It hurt. It cried, "Why don't you let me alone?" The owner said, "With your head dipped in a phosphorous solution you will be useful." So the little match had a head of phosphorus. A wonderful name was Phosphorous. It means in Greek, one who carries a light, a little Lightbearer. The match looked good. It said, "Now I am a little Lightbearer. I will occupy an important place."

It was put into a little box and there met fellow matches, little Lightbearers. They thought of great things that they would do. But it didn't work that way. They were put on a shelf in a store. The little one said to itself, "It doesn't seem that I have gained much. I once lived in a beautiful forest, with the sun shining, birds flying around, flowers at our feet, and the wind carrying a message of freedom. Now in a store, we hear only talk of business. We see only mercenary activities. We did not gain. There is no sap flowing. We are free in a way, each an individual match.

But what do we want of such freedom. How I wish we were back, but we cannot change destiny.

The little match became despondent. "What can I do now? I thought I could do great things; could light the world. Now I am in darkness. Will it ever come to an end?"

It was Christmas time. A woman came into the store and bought the box of matches. She took it home, and struck one of them. For the first time, it felt life again, just a little life. She lit a fire in the stove, and the fire became larger, and she cooked a meal for her family. Another match was lit, and with it a little candle on a Christmas tree was turned into a lovely, luminous candle, and people were happy. The match, though having paid with its life, was very happy. It said, "I never thought it would be so. Now that I have done this, my Soul is free, and my Soul will fly back to the forest, and will identify itself with the Soul of the big tree, and will never leave it again."

A man went to the same store and bought another box of matches. He went to his little cabin and lit a match to light his fire. He was intoxicated, and the match, without being extinguished, fell on the floor and set fire to the cabin, and the man perished. The poor match, dying suddenly, saw the disaster it caused. It said to itself, "I wanted to bring happiness, but I brought nothing but disaster. I will not go back to that little cabin. I never want to see any more disaster. Why did I ever leave my mother tree?"

Some matches can bring happiness, others destruction. When they were a part of the big tree, they did not have to pay with their lives to bring happiness. They did so, just by being a part of the big tree, indissolubly connected with it, enjoying all that the big tree enjoyed, spreading beauty, joy and happiness.

Each one of us who is a little match now, was once a part of that Great Trunk of Light. It wasn't good enough for us. We wanted to go on our own. We thought it would be easy. Our wishes took form in reality. We went through experiences. Finally we reached a condition where we could again enjoy life. Then we had again to wait, to have our heads plunged into phosphorous, a substance that could produce life. We had to make an effort. Some brought blessings, others nothing but destruction.

This is the lesson of life. It is up to us to choose because we have the power of discrimination. A match, which is lit, should give all in its power. When a match refuses to do all in its power, it blows out. So are we. We should never light a fire that is destructive. We should seemingly refuse our mission rather than turn it into a curse. We all see the big things. We do not realize that we can, with small effort, achieve big things. This is the tragedy of life.

Each one of us, on coming to Earth, is initiated to carry the Light. Each human is born that way. How few carry It as It should be carried. We have to stop and ponder. Especially at this period when we hear that beautiful statement of Peace on Earth, Good Will to Men. We should stop and think, is it really that way, or are we just a light in a fire of destruction.

There are two ways to live life, the right and the wrong way. To be on the fence is a loss to both sides. A New Year is soon coming to Humanity. What does it promise to Humanity? A great conflagration. It was started by individual matches. Instead of cheering up, lighting and warming the home, helping to get what we want in life, we just started the fire of conflagration.

How often children play with matches and cause no end of damage. It means that the match, humble as it is, is a great power for good or evil. The Light should not be used by people with minds of children, it should be used by grown up minds.

There are no little or big things. There is no division of little and big people. We have seen in historical times how a little match, a college boy assassinating an archduke, struck the flame of a war of unbelievable destruction, the First World War. We have seen another little match born in a humble cabin in the United States, when it was lit became the finest President the United States ever had, Abraham Lincoln.

Nobody is too little, nobody is too big. If we direct our activities properly, we can achieve big things. Others who seem to be big, direct their activities in the wrong direction and destroy the little things they could have achieved. It is all in our hands. It is not more difficult to do the right thing than the wrong thing. In fact it is easier because the Law of Harmony is with us. When we do the wrong thing, we have to fight against our Higher Self, our own interests and the interest of other people.

We go through life with eyes that do not see, ears that do not hear, senses that do not react as they should. We are blind to our path, deaf to the warning, and then a useless life. Humanity has proven this on the largest scale ever known, in our present condition. Just useless matches.

We are not responsible for others. We would like, in the spirit of good fellowship, to help them. We should try to do the best we can. Do we do it? No!

Humanity will not perish without fulfilling its mission to establish peace and happiness on Earth. It must some day reach its ultimate goal.

Why should Humanity live as they do for countless generations in the past and more in the future? One answer is human ignorance. In their blindness and stubbornness, they do not want to learn. There were countess lessons in the past, but they did not learn. They start all over again another lesson. The Seed of Truth and Enlightenment, falls on barren ground instead of on rich soil. The simple parable, given twenty centuries ago, teaches so well the life of Humanity.

When Jesus prayed in Gethsemane, "Father let this bitter cup pass from me," when he saw in vision the bitter cup he had to drink, said, "Not my will but Thy will be done. I will drink the cup." Those praying in churches now, want the cup to pass them by. They will have to drink it. Another group does not want to see the sorrows of others. They think they can avoid it. They cannot.

One can build within himself, the proper frame to stand and not to fall. We have this problem to face in the New Year. One cannot be honestly happy when the World is in so much sorrow, but we can see through their tears, some sun through the clouds. No matter how heavy the clouds are, some day they must go. Then the sun will fall on our life, will fill our life with true joy. We will know that life is the most glorious thing, the most wonderful adventure in the whole World.

We individual matches have to lie on the shelf a long time. Some day the time will come for us to do the right thing. That is what we Lightbearers are here for. We realize this to some extent. We want to live up to that mission from the Father. We want to return to the Home of the Great Universal Light. This is not religion or ethics, but just good common sense.

Lesson Forty-Two

STRENGTH AND COOPERATION

The whole condition of the World today is showing an unbelievable decline of strength – moral, mental and physical strength.

An elephant does not need to strengthen itself to fight tigers, or even humans. The elephant will face anything, but will not attack anything unless attacked. Then it will fight to the bitter end. Humans try to strengthen themselves with all kinds of mechanical devices, because they are weak. If we were really strong we would not need all the military armament of today, because our moral strength would influence the World. When morality is sustained, it imposes itself over everything and everyone.

Everything that humans have promulgated has something fundamentally taken from Nature. There is no isolation possible anywhere. Even worlds are connected by the Law of Attraction or Love. Sex is one of the channels through which Love manifests. Sexual attraction is being broken all the time among married people. Real Love cannot be broken.

There is no real partnership now on this Planet, except in very rare instances. The Lightbearers should try to create it among themselves. Without partnership there can be no peace, harmony, strength.

The reason fear is spreading all over the World is because people do not feel secure. We should find security at least when we come together in our Assemblies. It is not to learn more, that we are coming together. We already know so much that probably in hundreds of year the majority of people will not know as much as we now know.

We think some extraordinary power will help us. We should remember the saying, "Help yourself and Heaven will help you!" Moral strength is more important now than ever before, because mental strength may be on the decline. Nothing stimulates more than success, even in the wrong direction.

To accept wrong and not do anything about it, is moral cowardice. Animals when cornered will fight to the bitter end. It is only the perversion of the human mind that makes us think that we do not have courage. Yellow the color of the sun, has been perverted to mean a yellow streak, or a coward.

Strength is supported by cooperation. We are here to cooperate. If we have reached the higher state of life, though we actually dislike trouble, we are willing to share with others their trouble. We strengthen them and ourselves by sharing their troubles.

The World belongs to the conqueror, and the greatest conqueror is the one who conquers himself. We should see and sense all the wrong around us, but not be conquered by it.

Lesson Forty-Three

THANKSGIVING, 1950

Thanksgiving Day commemorates a very beautiful thought; more than that, a very beautiful feeling. The early settlers in this country had a very hard time, and often did not know which way to turn. When they got a little for their efforts, they turned to their Eternal father, and thus Thanksgiving Day was born, a day of thanks and love. There is nothing greater than to be thankful, first to the Eternal Father for His Love, and since all things come to us from The Father through human channels, our heart also goes to the channel. We should be grateful for what comes to us materially, mentally and emotionally.

It is very interesting to analyze the effects of gratitude. That inner love in it makes it possible for us to expand. There are very few emotions as strong, deep and beautiful as gratitude. The more grateful we will be, the more receptive we will be, and the more good things will come into our lives. It reminds us of that beautiful Commandment, "Love Thy Neighbor." Today the world is very, very selfish and hard. People think they have to become more and more selfish and hard in order to get along. Gratitude is Truth manifested and combined with Love. The present World has gone very far from Truth. It is very tragic that intelligent people should be so confused as to say that, since we are living in a world of lies, we must also be a liar. Where there are lies, there is no gratitude. A Liar is like a parasite which claims as its own that which does not belong to it. It is a very deplorable situation.

A sense of gratitude is embodied in everything living on this Planet. If we do not express it, we lose the best in life. Animals are always very grateful for all we do for them. When we water plants, they are so grateful that they unfold for us. That is what Mother Nature teaches us. Yet this beautiful instinct is more and more vanishing from the minds of people. We are now very near to the lowest point. Many people because of their pride say they will never accept help. They refuse because they do not want to be grateful they do not want to be under obligations. Some day they will learn their lessons, and will have to ask for help.

Gratitude makes us finer Beings. It pays to be grateful. They do not but there is a peculiar string attached to it. If we expect to get more of the same thing just because we are grateful of it, we will lose all that we are grateful for. A bird sings because its heart is full of love.

We are born with gratitude in us. Why should we now try to live without it? Thanksgiving Day each year reminds us of it, but very few people understand it. They think of a turkey dinner. How many are grateful to the turkey for giving its life? We are not grateful for all the things we receive from the Great Law through Its many channels. We only use the word "Thanks" just as a part of good form. Even this form is coming more and more out of use in modern generations. The beautiful Day of Thanksgiving has almost completely lost its deep meaning. People thank you and don't look at you while they are doing it. The eyes express more than words can express. If people had practiced in thought, feeling and deed the Principle of Gratitude, they would not be in the condition they are in today.

Ingratitude has so affected the elements that, instead of cooperating with us to produce our food and to give us a beautiful climate, they have become our enemies. Storms were not meant to destroy crops, or lightening to set fires. This was all brought about by a lack of gratitude. Let us remember to be thankful. Say, "Father, I Thank Thee," no matter what channel His Blessing flows through. Remember that every day of our lives should be a Thanksgiving Day. If we have troubles, we can by thankful that they are not worse, and that we have the possibility to rise above them.

Lesson Forty-Four

THE ADVENTURE OF LIFE

The word adventure is used nowadays almost in a way of contempt. People usually think of unsettled people. It seems to be the opposite of stability and security. This is not so. We often do not use the original meaning of words, using instead a meaning that is off color.

Ad, the first syllable of the word adventure, means to add to. Every moment we live there is an addition. Addition is represented by a balanced cross +. A balanced cross is a symbol of life. It is not a cross of agony or suffering. As it turns on its axis, it forms a circle. The first syllable of adventure is the unfoldment of life. Venture means to go on, to dare and do. It is an activity of a forward movement. Adventure is a forward movement, adding step by step, something new to our life.

We have to learn from the moment of birth to the end of life. Then there is another adventure through the Gate and into The Beyond. It is the mystery of life and the continual solution of the mystery. In adventure we never reach the final goal. If we did we would stop growing. In the adventure of life, we never know for sure what is going to happen. If we did, we would never use or develop all our qualities. Adventure always attracts us as a new mystery.

A child wants to see, then to touch, then to move, then to reason, and then to love. The same is true in the primitive aspect of life on Earth. Youth should want to see as much as they can of everything, and to see as deeply as they can. That is why our eyes contact about 80% of life. It is the most important sense we have. To see is not enough. We want to touch. Our hands and arms stand for ability to do things in life. We want to contact things with the idea of making something of them, that is, to make them move. Then our mind correlates what we see and touch. The better we correlate seeing and doing, the better off we will be.

Then we should love that which is worthwhile, and turn away from that which is not. If people followed this outline, life becomes more and more an interesting adventure. Then when we come to the Gates into The Beyond, we pass through, not with fear, but with an established feeling that the next step will be even more interesting and worthwhile. With such an attitude, no one will ever fear death.

In the Pagan symbolism of the Golden Age of Greece, this spirit was wide spread. The people loved life. That is why they produced the most beautiful buildings, sculpture, philosophies and science. We have not yet equaled them. We copy them and follow their political structures. They found life worth living, and had no fear of death. They faced the adventure of life beyond the gates.

This view of life as an adventure has been explained by all Avatars. Life at present is an extension of that at the time of Jesus. The ancient Greeks and primitive Christians were much alike. The early Christians were so successful that they brought about the fall of the Roman Empire, the greatest Empire in recorded history.

We find this same attitude in children. It is the way Nature intended it to be. People today do not respond in this way. We have lost the fundamental principle of the spirit of adventure. We have lost ourselves in details. In the Universe, the word adventure is written with stars as letters.

Fear is our handicap in the approach to life in the proper spirit. Fear is spreading more and more on this Planet. What people fear usually comes to them. Be without fear and without reproach in the adventure of life. In this, the opinion of no one else can be of value to us. Rely on our own judgment the best we know how. Our worst fear is to be afraid to dare and do. In other words to be afraid of life. A real adventurer never fails.

In life only real things count. Imitations or substitutes never count. There are no imitations in real life. They are only a product of a misdirected human mind. Life now is an ever increasing foolishness, based on fear and resulting in confusion. Fearless people are wise people. We cannot live wisdom without courage. We are afraid of wisdom. Foolishness seems so much easier. No human can be important who is full of fear. He remains just a shadow. How can a shadow meet the realities of life? It cannot.

We are now facing some of the hardest realities Humanity has ever seen. We have hardly started yet what is in store for us in the days to come. We must be a true adventurer, without fear and without reproach.

Lesson Forty-Five

THE STRONGEST TEST OF LIGHTBEARERS

Do not doubt in our Teachings, and do not become disloyal to them. When Jesus was reviled and crucified, they were disloyal to Him. He brought them the Truth that was meant to set them free. The Jews will continue to pay for this until they recognize their mistake. When one of them does recognize it, he will be born in the next incarnation in the body of a Gentile.

Sometimes test are so great and our minds so befogged, that we do not know what we are doing. A betrayal that is not atoned for starts a new cause based on betrayal. When a person suffers enough, he will be relieved of the Law of Cause and Effect in that respect. Spies are shot for betrayal of their country. Betrayal of a Principle is greater than betrayal of a country.

Trust is based on Truth, which is a Law. If the Law is betrayed, the whole Universe will collapse. Fortunately a Spiritual Law cannot be betrayed.

The concept of friendship does not exist in the United States. Instead it is either sex or money. People have transgressed the fundamental Principle of Friendship and Loyalty. Some day they will realize this, but it will be too late. There is no loyalty now between husband and wife, between parents and children, between labor and management, between physicians and their oath of Hippocrates, between judges and their duty, between lawyers and their conscious, between trade, commerce and production and its customers. We live in a mental atmosphere of disloyalty. This is why it is so difficult now to be loyal.

Those who are disloyal suffer not only for the rest of this incarnation but also in The Beyond, and most of all, in the next incarnation. One of the simple ways to learn to be loyal is to keep ones promises.

TODAY AND TOMORROW

In the Realm of Harmony there is only today. It is very questionable if we will ever reach that stage. It means All; nothing of yesterday and nothing of tomorrow, All Today. Only the Infinite can cover All. As we approach that stage, today will begin to merge with tomorrow.

Some people have their feet firmly entrenched on the ground. They are successful people. Others are floating in mid-air. These are unsuccessful. They must someday come to Earth as birds do. It will be like being thrown back to the Earth, and they will hit very hard. The blow will be in direct proportion to how high they are in the air. This is called the hard-knocks of life. They have been living too much in tomorrow.

Today is the time we must do everything that has to be done today. Some things are to be done tomorrow, because mind can extend itself to tomorrow in the planning. However, the accomplishments are only today, never tomorrow. We must learn to prepare ourselves to do the things of today, to become elastic for tomorrow's duties. A mind that is frozen loses its elasticity.

Life is not something unexpected, not a surprise, not something coming out of a clear sky. It is a series of manifestations of the operation of the Law of Cause and Effect. Life is directed in a way by Destiny, so that all parts fit together. We must do now what must be done now, because we start a cause which will cause an effect. Since most things affect other people, the effect must be harmonious.

The Great Law is the Conductor of the Orchestra of the Life Symphony of the human race. Each of us must play our own notes. The Great Conductor has written the Symphony with all the parts for each of us to play. It is very unfortunate that we do not consider the notes we have to play, but pay too much attention to the notes of others around us. One of the greatest interferences with our harmonious living is to postpone until tomorrow what is to be done today. Procrastination is our greatest mistake. Doing does not mean only to move things. That is very primitive. It is more important to say the right thing at the right time. When we have an urge to say something and do not say it, we often produce the greatest mistakes for ourselves and for others. We should learn to be silent when we should be silent, and to speak when we should speak. When we have to do something or say something, it is because the Law of Cause and Effect forces us to do it.

Many people, instead of being guided by their own reasoning, are guided by the reasoning of other people. This often creates mass thinking, which in turn expresses itself in mob hysteria. We now have a mob hysteria connected with the atomic bomb. This will probably cause an explosion. We should listen to other people's thoughts, but not be influenced by them. We have today mob hysteria developed to an extraordinary degree. In the United States we have mass production of everything, including mass thinking. We should not be influenced by mass thinking unless it agrees with our own thinking.

When the intelligence of high class individuals is functioning on this Planet, these people pull the others in their direction. Today the minds of people are beginning to unfold, so as to think individually. So they are not so much affected by the wrong reasoning of others. They think for themselves. Unfortunately this is not yet strong enough to oppose wrong leadership. In other countries it became strong enough, and as a result, there was the French Revolution and the Russian Revolution. The same will happen in the United States.

As a general rule Humanity is now on a much higher level than even fifty years ago. Today everything, especially change, is drastic. We should not be led astray by others, but we should be guided by our own mind. When we break away from wrong thinking of others, we have a terrible reaction. We should have a mental mask.

Every person has an inborn sense of balance. This is also true of the whole Creation. If we have this physically, we must also have it mentally and spiritually. Teachers should help us to learn to help ourselves mentally, as the mother bird teaches its young to fly. We must develop a mental judgment of what others say, so that we will instinctively know whether or not it is right. We should not accept it blindly.

Do today all that we can do today, in the order that things come to us to do and by and by, things will adjust for us. If we look into our own lives, we can learn very important lessons by remembering the past and seeing our shortcomings. We can see, by not starting the right cause, we got the wrong effect. We should not let something interfere with doing a thing when it should be done. There is a way to do it, because the demand for doing it would never come, if there were not a way. We do not trust this Law.

Today has never seen tomorrow, but it has an advantage over both tomorrow and yesterday because today can think of both yesterday and tomorrow. We should remember the past, and think of the future, but live in the present. We have no power over the past, but it can be of tremendous value to us by remembering both our mistakes and our successes. The notebook of our memory of the past gives us the knowledge of how something worked out. It will work the same way today, if we hesitate to do something today, look at a similar condition in the past and see how it worked then. Most of us are not guided by our reason, but by our fears or by our desires.

The future is non-existent except in our thoughts and in the operation of the Law of Cause and Effect. The effect is in the future. After we do the best we can today, we should not worry, but leave the future to the Eternal Law of Cause and Effect. The effect of a word or act may be very far-reaching. When once started, it cannot be withdrawn. We are today building our future every moment of our lives. There is no use to be sorry or mortify ourselves about mistakes, but let them be red lights to stop us from making the same mistake again.

Since we live on Earth only a comparatively short time, most people do not realize that effects often come in future incarnations. Our present life, not only reaps the rewards of past incarnations, but we plant the seeds of future lives. It is not wise just to live today and not plan for tomorrow. But the plans must not be too definite. The Planning should be elastic. Don't worry about tomorrow, because the Law of Cause and Effect infallibly works. We often want to anticipate or figure out how things will come out. Polarity usually causes the opposite from what we anticipate.

We should in our own work, take into consideration the pulse of Humanity. The pulse of the World, right now, is beating at an extraordinary speed. It is speeding towards an end of some kind. Hurry never brings good results. Hurrying is different from being quick. Some people are naturally quick, and others naturally slow. Slow people should not be lazy. Those who are slow but steady, usually in an emergency achieve great feats. We should make the best use of our own nature, but not be in a hurry.

Lesson Forty-Seven

TRADITIONS AND CONVENTIONS

We cannot disregard that which is good just because it is old, and we cannot disregard a new thing if it is good. Some traditions are almost as old as thinking Humanity, and are still good. When traditions have fulfilled what is expected of them, they should be dropped.

The FourSquare Principle was before Humanity was. There never was a time when It did not exist, and there never will be a time when It will not exist. Such a Principle must be the foundation of all traditions and conventions. We should be on the conservative side. We should not oppose traditions and conventions until after we have analyzed them. We cannot standardize everything. Giving one's age seems to put one in that age class. It puts him in a straight jacket, damaging him and cutting away his freedom. I enjoyed, when young, the company of old people because I could learn from them. The youth of my day did not know half of the things present day youths know, but they were more mature.

Democracy in the United States is said to be developing respect of one another. There is less respect here than in other countries. There can be no respect without Love, and no Love without respect.

Things that create impressions can never be forgotten. Impressions received when young are much deeper than when older. Children trust their parents and trust the World. We should learn through unfoldment, through the advantage the thing has on the person doing it. This must be a threefold advantage, physical, mental and Spiritual. A Spiritually unfolded person sees Divinity in everything, even a blade of grass. The more Spiritual a person, the more compassionate he is, the more charitable he is in all that he does.

Lesson Forty-Eight

TRANSMUTATION

There is no such thing literally as a transmutation. The so-called ones are not transmutation. If atoms are added to elements, it is not a transmutation, but a creation of a new element, which has something, added. The so-called science of medieval times called it transmutation. In scientific language, words unfortunately are not always used exactly as they should be.

What's right is right and what's wrong is wrong. I admit that in my younger days, I frequently used the word "transmute" but I never said that wrong could be transmuted to right. Sometimes wrong seems to be transmuted to right, but this is not so. It remains wrong until it is destroyed.

Evil may regenerate itself. If the individual is evil, he will be reborn evil until he changes his rate of vibration. The right kind of vibration must be substituted, then the wrong vibrations dies. Evil must have an end. Good will never has an end, because it never started. It always existed. Evil because it has in it the seed of death is with each birth growing shorter, although it may be very virulent at times. No religion, except the Christian, has proclaimed the Eternity of Hell or evil.

The Higher Self is really the inner structure around which our body is woven. It is perfect unity. It is our FourSquare, a combination of Mind and Love supported by Life and Law. These qualities of the FourSquare constitute Divinity or our Father. In the Story of Creation, God created male and female. Male means Mind, Female means Love. The two are indissolubly connected, the Heavenly Twins.

We may use instead of transmutation, the word "liberation". Good can be liberated from evil. Evil is like dirt around good. Evil would like to be liberated from good, but it cannot be. It must submit to good. Good will always win the final victory, because it is without beginning and without end. When good is liberated, the evil is destroyed. From evil, no good comes. It is always there. We cannot hobnob with evil and forget it is evil. If we must be with evil for a while, we should do so only to try to get rid of it.

In Science of Being, page 319, we find, "Thus the veils of self-delusion will be withdrawn one by one, limitations will be removed, suffering conquered, sorrow transmuted into Joy". I wrote this before I realized completely the meaning of the word "transmute". I should have said, "Sorrow replaced by Joy". Sorrow cannot be transmuted into joy. It may vanish, disintegrate and give place to joy. In the midst of sorrow, joy can be born, like good seeds germinating among the tares. Joy increases and increases and sorrow must go. Evil, like darkness, is destroyed by light. Darkness cannot destroy light. It can invade light, if the light is diminishing. If we want to get rid of anything wrong, we must increase the right, and by and by the wrong will disappear.

An individual, who increases his concept of good, decreases his attitude to be affected by wrong. The best immunization of an individual to germs is to become self immune by Nature. Immunity is the conquest of good over evil. It is replacement. Evil is replaced by good. Evil is not ever present and omnipotent, because, if so, there would be no hope for Humanity. Evil is by no means a power to which we should attribute the word "conquer'. The best way is to dismiss it. Say – "Get behind me".

Everything wrong is a parasite. We supply the parasites with vitality. When there is an explosion of the wrong, we discover the good was always there. We needed our mental or emotional eyes opened.

When we get so disgusted with so much evil, our Higher Self impels us to seek something good. Man's extremity is God's opportunity. When we have reached the ultimate in endurance of something wrong, we want to be reunited with right. When we are sick and tired of evil, of wrong, of lies, we turn ourselves to the very reverse.

We should synchronize ourselves with every little good. Try to rise above evil and unite with all that is good. Try to increase our storage of good. Then will come a change in us, which will seem like a transmutation.

Lesson Forty-Nine

THE LAW OF RETRIBUTION

Why are we having so many accidents now with airplanes? It is surprising the number of people being killed recently, especially civilians. We must remember that no thought, word, feeling or action is ever lost. Sooner or later it will come back. This is the Law of Cause and Effect. There is no possible way to redeem it, except by paying the penalty.

This Country was founded on peace and good will toward men. As long as we lived up to such Principles as much as we mortals can, there was comparatively relative peace. Extraordinary prosperity, high moral standards. The people were known to be very generous in an intelligent way. They minded their own business, which is one of the fundamental laws. Also people were strong physically, mentally and morally. So this Country became an example to follow, an inspiration to the rest of the world. Now we are getting back all that we did. Our airplanes attacked civilians in cities. The fundamental principles of this country were violated. The latest Boeing crash is exactly what we did in Germany and Japan. In ancient days wars were based on a fair fight not on killing helpless civilians from the air.

The United States Constitution was supposed to give Humanity a new country in which to live. We have now so lost our sense of right that we put an individual above a Principle. The evangelist, Billy Graham, advocates the personality of Jesus above the Principles of Life. He says to surrender yourself to Jesus. This is a deplorable failure in an attempt, which could have done so much. Jesus was nothing but a channel, a great channel, a wonderful Channel.

The only redemption that counts is through our own self and not through another, even though he was a great channel. There must be a long struggle and preparation within the individual before there can be any sudden redemption. It cannot be done in a moment of emotional outburst, but as a result of a conviction. To dedicate one's life to the personality of Jesus means the greatest sacrifice. To dedicate it to the Principles of Jesus would be a wonderful thing. This requires a very serious consideration.

When we lived in the Realm of Harmony, we had the Law of Reward. When we fell from that Realm, we changed the Law of Reward, to the Law of Retribution. The Law of Reward is an Eternal Law. The Law of Retribution is not an Eternal Law. It is like the shadow of the Law of Reward. The Law of Retribution works both on the Physical plane and in the Beyond. There is no escape from it. Both the Law of Retribution and the Law of Reward, increase as they come back to us.

Since time immemorial, all the Great Teachers have taught the Law of Retribution. We Humans know it exceptionally well without knowing it is a Law. We know that what we plant we reap. This works in every line of activity. If we start a thing wrongly, we not only cannot obtain the right results, but the more we work on it, the worse it gets. Humans do not want to accept such a self evident proposition.

The situation seems to be hopeless, because we all without exception are in the wrong. We must first recognize that we are wrong. The tolerance of wrong is the most destructive attitude towards life itself. We should say, "I made a mistake and I will try to do the right thing." Right will automatically counterbalance the wrong and win over it.

We must change our attitude of mind if we want to produce something better – the change must come from within us. Then the Law of Retribution will become the Law of Reward.

Lesson Fifty

THE UNMANIFEST

The Eternal is often referred to as the Unmanifest. We also speak of His Manifestations. Probably because of the depth of these words, most people do not understand their meaning. Unmanifest means that which is unknown. We cannot know that which did not come in some way into manifestation. The Eternal is and forever will be, Unknown. Unless we think, our power of thinking remains unmanifest. A manifestation on the mental plane is not sufficient. It must also be manifested on the physical plane. It must be translated from the mental to the physical. That which is manifested, is that which we can from every angle approach and understand. It can be approached and understood from each of the three planes.

The Eternal eternally manifests out of Its unmanifest condition. Through the manifested World, we by and by, learn more and more about the unmanifest, which is ruling its own manifestation. We will never reach the fullness of the unmanifest and never the fullness of the manifestation. Neither the Spiritual nor the physical Universe can expand, but our mental concept can and does expand. This continual revelation will go on throughout Eternity, which never started. We have created endless revelations in the Past, but we have forgotten them.

Lesson Fifty-One

WILL POWER

When we use too much will power, it is a clear indication of limitations. We should stop when we have had enough. When the point of saturation is reached, we cannot go beyond it. When this point is reached, since we are continually expanding, expansion takes place, and the next time we can do more. In studying, when we have reached the limit, we must stop. If we use will power to do more, we contract. Then next time, we will stop before the last time.

We are all without exception, born lazy. Laziness is a form of stupor, which is normal for subconsciousness. Subconsciousness is doped. Within us is vitality or life, which represents our Higher Self. The more we let It come to the surface, the more we win the battle, but it has a limit when we must stop and recuperate. The urge of the Higher Self is the conquering power, but, for the time being, we are a limited human being. Though we are using an unlimited power. Faith and enthusiasm is the highest emotional power we can get, and it relaxes us.

No constructive effort can ever produce an undesirable effect. However, some great artists have destroyed themselves by having an unreasonable ambition. A feverish ambition destroys an individual. A balanced ambition improves one. We should not try to outdo or outlive our own glory.

A fundamental trait of each being is to be friendly. This is so even with animals. Wild animals, which have never seen humans, are friendly when they meet them, if the humans are not afraid of them.

There is always a distinction between right and wrong, but each person will interpret a thing differently. People, who lose their concept of right and wrong, use alibis. They are not sane. That is why the World is in such a terrible condition, because it is full of alibis. Sanity is balance. We should never use alibis.

People in the United States are unbelievable emotional. That is why we have so much heart trouble. Continuous talkers are least subject to heart trouble. To be always silent usually means a great repression. To find out what people's real emotions are, we must penetrate very deeply into their minds. An instinctive response is a true one. Premeditated action is not sincere action. Instinct belongs to the Higher Self in spite of most psychologists. The instinct of birds to build a nest is from the Higher Self. Destructive things come from the lower self. Human mothers will leave their children, but animal mothers never will. This comes from the Higher Self of the animal, whereas the human mother is influenced by her lower self.

With most of us there is, through long training, a habit of self control. Modern psychologists advise not to repress, but to express. If we express and explosion within us, which damages others, we are injured ourselves. Some people are naturally kind. Some try to be kind when they are not. Some take a fanatical attitude in trying to be kind. They are insincere. There are times when we must be unkind. Truth should never be an insult anyone. To be good means to be wholeheartedly one with that which is good.

The greatest crime of the human mind is to have unblocked the secrets of creation and used them for destructive purposes in the atomic bomb, rather than to help people. We stole the secrets from Nature. We are a gang of thieves. The United States was leader of the gang. The scientists thought they did a great patriotic thing. They lost their sense of right and wrong. At one time in the Past, we did not know the difference between right and wrong. The legend of the Garden of Eden refers to that time. Children do not know the difference and have to be trained. A stern expression in parents affects them more than words. Animals can be easily controlled by a stern expression.

We learn through suffering more than any other way. Animals learn in the same way. There is nothing worse than to betray someone. We will never be able to contact our Higher Self if we block ourselves to It. We should never use alibis. The only road to the Higher Self, is the direct road. By facing our Higher Self, we face the Eternal, and by facing the Eternal, we face our Higher Self.

Lesson Fifty-Two

WHAT IS GOD?

God is All Life, Intelligence, Law and Love. He is the Life, which sustains the whole Universe, the Intelligence, which guides the whole Universe, the Law, which protects the whole Universe, and the Love, which holds together everything in a sense of Harmony.

The Father of the Universe is the One who Creates, Constitutes, Governs, Sustains and contains All. The word God does not mean anything to a person unless he has a preconceived idea of it. The Masons call God, the Great Architect, the Great Builder.

It is difficult in present world conditions to believe there is a God. Yet we must believe that the fundamental Principles of Life exists. Plants in the Spring are regenerated. Science has proven there is energy, and energy is Life. Everything in the Universe pulsates, or moves, and that is Life. Life is a word coined by us to explain the functioning of energy. Energy is the foundation of life, and is Life. No one can deny there is an extraordinary Intelligence, which has constituted everything in its place. No one can deny, even in this lawless community, which we call Humanity that Law does not exist. Laws cannot be abolished. We have to recognize them. All evil in this world is due to violation of Laws. This violation causes friction, and in friction there is always loss. Proper working of Laws has no friction. Laws still work, but we are not in tune with them. The Power, which we call, Love is sustaining us, holding us together. Remove the Power from our body, and the body dies. Remove It from our heart and we become cold, hard-hearted.

We cannot explain the Unexplainable in a way. We must approach It from all sides. The concept of God is so colossal that our human mind can only touch a fraction of it. The word Infinity means no end. Modern people are so sophisticated, so complicated, that they want complicated answers. The simplest things are usually the greatest.

No Being, no Spirit will ever understand Infinity and Eternity. Only Infinity KNOWS Itself, and Infinity is God. Also, Eternity is God. If we were to finally grasp God, then we would merge with God. The the whole of Eternity, we will always be exploring God, and learning more of It. This will always be very interesting.

Lesson Fifty-Three

WHAT IS SCIENCE?

Webster defines Science as organized knowledge. That is the best definition of science. When knowledge is not organized, it is not science.

When a bird builds a nest, it uses its Higher Self to build the nest where it should be and how it should be. The bird uses knowledge, but it cannot really be called science, because the bird is not consciously aware of doing it this way. The Superconciousness in plants awakens in the seed the stimulus to grow. Subconsciousness in anything does not want it to grow.

Science is that knowledge which we feel is correct and organized. Science of Being means organized knowledge of existence. It includes the FourSquare Principle, including Spirit and Its counterpart Matter. When we live the FourSquare, we are both spiritual and material, successful on the physical, mental and emotional planes.

Eternal Existence is already organized, completed from Eternity. The Eternal cannot add anything to It. It will never be completely revealed to us. This will furnish the interest, stimulus and variety of living. Only the Eternal KNOWS ALL. It broadens Itself through us, greater and greater in every direction.

Science of Being is the perfect understanding of everything. We will never be able to learn today what we should learn tomorrow. If we could, there would be a missing link. If there were a missing link, it would be disorganized. Human science is in almost all cases, very inaccurate. Mathematics is probably the exception.

The whole Universe is based on science, and science is the FourSquare. If we do anything the FourSquare way, we do it scientifically.

We cannot improve our Higher Self. We can give It the opportunity to express Itself. Our Higher Self Knows All that God Knows, and has known all throughout all Eternity. It is not The All, but a Ray of All. It will never come to the end of knowing Itself. It will always be progressing. This is very difficult for the human mind to understand. There will always be an increased feeling of expanding inside. "Know Thy Self and Thou Shalt Know All."

Lesson Fifty-Four

WHY ARE WE BORN?

This is the question, which is asked by people when things go wrong. Some say we are born in order to die. This is a very sad answer, but we cannot deny that so-called death is the outcome for every human being. According to legend, some prophets, including Enoch, passed through translation without death. They are said to have raised the rate of vibration of the body until it disappeared. This would seem to be the exception to the rule, but we have no proof that such exceptions ever took place.

There must be an end whenever there is a beginning. A wrong in our lives must have an end because it had a beginning. The same is true of a good.

There is in youth an urge to live, a buoyancy, and optimistic attitude toward life. This is like plants in the Spring. Then comes maturity when we survey the field of wheat ready for harvest. Then comes Fall when we rest in more or less inactivity. Then winter, the end, the sleep. This has been accepted by Humanity for countless generations.

Rejuvenation is actually going on continuously in the body. If our minds would let it work, we would live for at least 250 years. Then our interests would shift to a higher level, interest which could not be satisfied on this plane.

Modern civilization has made out of humans a mechanical unit. Scientists and doctors look upon a human as a machine. A machine cannot rejuvenate itself. It has to be done from the outside. Humans can do it from the inside. Nothing in Nature stops unfolding. Humans, since they are a part of Nature, are no exception. Long lived people are close to Nature. Old age without vigor is one of the greatest punishments. Most people today go through this. The human mind is unbelievably powerful in the human body. Humanity is afraid of its own shadow. When completely surrounded by Light or knowledge, there is no shadow.

Who made death seem so terrible? It cannot be blamed on religions. They try to make it a very interesting experience. Scientists and psychologists are responsible. A doctor can only tell a person that the end has come. He has nothing else to tell. It is the same with physiologists.

People are more afraid of death than of anything else. If people had lived as they should the repair work would have been done from within and not from without, as the doctors attempted to do. We are not born to die, but to live, and we also die to live. We are born for continual unfoldment of life. If humans were not so limited by the lack of proper knowledge, they would live and make as much out of life as possible. Then they would unfold from within.

Most people grow kinder as they grow older, also broader, finer, more spiritual, more appreciative of kindness. They are glad to give and give. They prepare themselves for a change. Then they are ready to pass on with a lovely expression. Translation is very easy. Young people can never enjoy life properly. They think they can. It requires a mature mind.

We are not here to come to the end and be afraid of what is next. Light is Truth. With faces set to The Light, we can understand the real meaning of life. We should use our power to do something right and not to fight something wrong. We have within us that inextinguishable Light. It remains with us all our life and It is the only thing we take into The Beyond.

Let us send to sufferers thoughts of Love. Love is not human. It is a Spark of the Eternal of which we are the Bearer.

Lesson Fifty-Five

WHERE IS THE BEYOND?

All we can say, and all the Great Teachers of the Past could say, is that it is Beyond. This does not explain it at all. There have been thousands of books written trying to explain it. The authors did not know.

The Great Teachers only said that it would be very peaceful for those who deserve it, but just the opposite for those who do not deserve it. The peacefulness will be different for each person.

It is very difficult for us materially minded people to believe that we will have a body, a mind and the emotional side all represented. But this will be so. Yet we will not be material Entities as we are now. It is really impossible for one to figure it out. That is why people were given a fictitious idea of life beyond. One interpretation is that we will go where we belong according to our rate of vibration. We do not know what our own rate of vibration is. This is why we still study ourselves.

Many people are entering The Beyond now not due to old age, but to war, accidents, etc. An accident, even the dropping of a dish, is not normal. Even if we forget something it shows that our normality is below par. It shows our Higher Self is not working as it should. If we are open to our Higher Self, we would never forget anything.

Millions of people are in a category below normal. We should admit there is something wrong within us. When a distressed world condition is becoming as manifest as it is today, we should try to counteract it in our own mind. Those who today are guiding the Destiny of Humanity are opening the Gates of The Beyond very wide. The worst offenders are the scientists. They are developing the atomic bombs. To use a constructive Force of Nature, against the Children of Nature, is one of the greatest crimes. The earlier weapons of warfare were of a low standing. Atomic Energy is a Sacred Power.

The Gate of The Beyond is one gate. We will all pass through that one gate, but the minute we pass through, we will face a crossroad. Those vibrating low will take the wrong road. Those vibrating high will take the right road. There will be no St. Peter there, nor any other Entity. It will work automatically, according to the Law. Some are led to do the wrong thing now. This shows there is something wrong with us. We do not vibrate to Truth. A lie is more predominant or prevalent in us. It will continue to be the same in The Beyond. There will be no sudden adjustment. The Beyond is beyond our human calculations. We should place ourselves in the hands of the Great Law. It will not desert us in The Beyond.

At the time of passing, our whole life in this incarnation passes in review. We remember everything. Many people have had the experience, when they nearly passed out, of remember all, and then coming back. I had this experience while swimming in the ocean.

In our Spiritual Lesson, the Flame shows very well our passing. When It is first lighted it burns very low. This represents our physical life on this plane. The Flame is transmuted which corresponds to our passing. Then It grows larger in size and becomes translucent, ethereal and with beautiful colors. This is a symbol of what will happen in The Beyond. Some will be just a little flicker of a flame. Some will be very much changed. The last flame in Seattle was the most beautiful one I have ever seen.

We should take our passing in a philosophical way. Nothing can stop it. It may happen any day. We should say, "Why should I worry, I cannot change it." The more we worry, the more we spoil the remainder of our life on this plane.

Criminals who are executed usually ask for a minister. The so-called absolution of their sins only acts as a dope for them. When they awaken in The Beyond, they will be in great mental agony. It will be much better for them to go through a few seconds of unbelievable agony, a mental picture of Hell. This would atone much more for their crimes than a clergyman. For their own good, the last consolation of religions should be denied them.

In passing we should say, "Father in Thy Hands, I am placing my Life."

The Commandment of
THE LIGHTBEARERS to the World

> **"BE MAN"—Express in every act of yours All ENERGY, INTELLIGENCE, TRUTH and LOVE; thus Living only will you live; thus acting only can you build to Freedom, Strength and Happiness in Life. This is your Problem: be this your Foremost Aim.**

The Commandment! Throughout the whole of Eternity there will never be another Commandment given. THE LIGHTBEARERS Commandment is that great. The FourSquare is the essence of Truth. It covers the ground so completely, that even God, if He wanted to improve It, He could not do so. It was the foundation of Creation, throughout all Eternity, and will continue so for Eternity. The Infinite Intelligence opened my eyes to see the logical sequence of the Four Corners. If we have faith that the FourSquare is all there is, we are open to the Eternal. If we have no faith, we close the door to the Eternal.

~Eugene Fersen ~

"Vibrations"

Father, I am Thy Individualized Projection into Thine Own Eternal substance proceeding from Thee, indissolubly connected with Thee, manifesting all Thy Qualities and Powers. I am indeed the image and likeness of Thee.

Mother, I am Thy Individualized Projection into Thine Own Eternal substance proceeding from Thee, indissolubly connected with Thee, manifesting all Thy Qualities and Powers. I am indeed the image and likeness of Thee.

Great Eternal One — The Creator of the Universe, I Thy created am Thy Individualized Projection into Thine Own Eternal substance proceeding from Thee, indissolubly connected with Thee, manifesting all They Qualities and Powers. I am indeed the image and likeness of Thee.

Divine Mother, Love Eternal, I, Thy child am Thy Individualized Projection into Thine Own Eternal substance proceeding from Thee, indissolubly connected with Thee, manifesting all Thy Qualities and Powers. I am indeed the image and likeness of Thee.

And, as such, I am open on the physical plane to the influx of Divine Wisdom, Infinite Abundance and Limitless Supply.

And, on the Mental Plane my mind is open to the influx of Divine Wisdom and Thy Limitless Supply.

And on the Plane of Spirit forever is my Soul open to the influx of Divine Wisdom, Eternal Love and Limitless Supply.

And this realization comes down to the Mental Plane.

And on down to my everyday life where I KNOW I am open to the influx of Divine Wisdom, Divine Abundance and Limitless Supply.

Father, Thou are inspiring me on the Spiritual Plane. Thou art guiding me on the Mental Plane. Thou art sustaining and protecting me on the Physical Plane.

Made in United States
Orlando, FL
22 March 2024

45054800R00140